LAST LOOKS, LAST BOOKS

LAST LOOKS, LAST BOOKS

Stevens, Plath, Lowell, Bishop, Merrill

Helen Vendler

THE A. W. MELLON LECTURES IN THE FINE ARTS, 2007
NATIONAL GALLERY OF ART, WASHINGTON
BOLLINGEN SERIES XXXV: 56

Princeton University Press
Princeton and Oxford

Published by Princeton University Press, 41 William Street,
Princeton, New Jersey 08540
In the United Kingdom: Princeton University Press,
6 Oxford Street, Woodstock, Oxfordshire OX20 1TW

This is the fifty-sixth volume of the A. W. Mellon Lectures in the Fine Arts, which
are delivered annually at the National Gallery of Art, Washington. The volumes
of lectures constitute Number XXXV in Bollingen Series, sponsored by the
Bollingen Foundation.

Requests for permission to reproduce material from this work
should be sent to Permissions, Princeton University Press

Owing to limitations of space, acknowledgments of permissions to use previously
published material will be found at the back of the book.

Vendler, Helen, 1933-
Last looks, last books : Stevens, Plath, Lowell, Bishop, Merrill / Helen Vendler.
p. cm. — (The A.W. Mellon lectures in the fine arts ; 2007) (Bollingen series ;
XXXV, 56)
ISBN 978-0-691-14534-1 (cloth : alk. paper)   1. American poetry—
20th century—History and criticism.   2. Death in literature.   I. Title.
PS310.D42V46 2010
811'.5093548—dc22   2009039549

British Library Cataloging-in-Publication Data is available

This book has been composed in Adobe Jenson Pro

Printed on acid-free paper. ∞

press.princeton.edu

Printed in the United States of America

3   5   7   9   10   8   6   4   2

FOR DAVID, MY BELOVED AND STEADFAST SON

Onely a sweet and virtuous soul,
Like season'd timber, never gives;
But though the whole world turn to coal,
Then chiefly lives.

—GEORGE HERBERT

Contents

Acknowledgments

I am grateful to all those at the National Gallery of Art who honored me by the invitation to give the Mellon Lectures of 2007 and by their personal kindness to me during the period of the lectures: Earl A. Powell III, Director of the Gallery; Elizabeth Cropper, Dean of the Center for Advanced Study in the Visual Arts; Therese O'Malley, Associate Dean of CASVA; David Brown; and Andrew Drabkin. I enjoyed very much not only the presentation of the lectures but also the social occasions surrounding them, as well as the seminar with the Fellows of CASVA.

As I wrote these lectures, I profited from month-long residencies at the National Humanities Center (the Assad Meymandi Residency) and the American Academy of Berlin. I thank Dr. Meymandi; Geoffrey Harpham, Director of the National Humanities Center; Kent Mullikin, Executive Director of the Humanities Center; and Gary Smith, Executive Director of the American Academy of Berlin for their generous welcome. I was aided in writing these lectures not only by my compensation as Mellon Lecturer but also by research funds from the Department of English at Harvard (the Hyder Rollins Fund) and from my research fund as a University Professor.

I thank Steven Yenser of UCLA for our conversation about James Merrill's difficult poem, "The Instilling."

I am indebted to Kristin Lambert, my assistant, for continued help in preparing the final manuscript, and to Hanne Winarsky of Princeton University Press for helping this book into print. I also thank Ellen Foos and Dalia Geffen at Princeton.

LAST LOOKS, LAST BOOKS

1

Introduction: Last Looks, Last Books

There is a custom in Ireland called "taking the last look." When you find yourself bedridden, with death approaching, you rouse yourself with effort and, for the last time, make the rounds of your territory, North, East, South, West, as you contemplate the places and things that have constituted your life. After this last task, you can return to your bed and die. W. B. Yeats recalls in letters how his friend Lady Gregory, dying of breast cancer, performed her version of the last look. Although for months she had remained upstairs in her bedroom, three days before she died she arose from her chair—she had refused to take to her bed—and painfully descended the stairs, making a final circuit of the downstairs rooms before returning upstairs and finally allowing herself to lie down. And Yeats himself, a few years later, took his last look in a sonnet called "Meru," which cast a final glance over all his cultural territory: "Egypt and Greece, good-bye, and good-bye, Rome!"

In many lyrics, poets have taken, if not a last look, a very late look at the interface at which death meets life, and my topic is the strange binocular style they must invent to render the reality contemplated in that last look. The poet, still alive but aware of the imminence of death, wishes to enact that deeply shadowed but still vividly alert moment; but how can the manner of a poem do justice to both the looming presence of death and the unabated vitality of spirit? Although death is a frequent theme in European literature, any response to it used to be fortified by the belief in a personal afterlife. Yet as the conviction of the soul's afterlife waned, poets had to invent what Wallace Stevens called "the mythology of modern death." In the pages that follow, I take the theme of death and the genre of elegy as given and focus instead on the problem of style in poems confronting not death in general, nor the death of someone else, but personal extinction. I draw my chief examples of such poetry from the last books of some modern American poets: Wallace Stevens, Sylvia Plath, Robert Lowell, Elizabeth Bishop, and James Merrill. The last books of other American poets—John Berryman, A. R. Ammons—could equally well have been chosen, but the poems I cite illustrate with particular distinction both the rewards and the hazards of presenting life and death as mutually, and demandingly, real within a single poem's symbolic system.

Before I come to describe pre-modern practice in such poems, I want to illustrate very briefly in two poets, Stevens and Merrill, what I mean by "the problem of style" in a poem that wishes to be equally fair to both life and death at once. Both poets show style as powerfully diverted from expected norms by the stress of approaching death. The first of these poems is by Wallace Stevens, and it is called "The Hermitage at the Center." (Even its title is baffling; the poem has no hermitage and no hermit, at least at first glance):

THE HERMITAGE AT THE CENTER

The leaves on the macadam make a noise—
How soft the grass on which the desired
Reclines in the temperature of heaven—

Like tales that were told the day before yesterday—
Sleek in a natural nakedness,
She attends the tintinnabula—

And the wind sways like a great thing tottering—
Of birds called up by more than the sun,
Birds of more wit, that substitute—

Which suddenly is all dissolved and gone—
Their intelligible twittering
For unintelligible thought.

And yet this end and this beginning are one,
And one last look at the ducks is a look
At lucent children round her in a ring.[1]

Stevens has here presented a poem that seems unintelligible as one reads it line by line. It contains, as we eventually realize, two poems that have been interdigitated—one of death, one of life, converging in a joint coda. The first poem—that of death, of seasonal end, of unintelligible extinction—can be seen by reading in succession the opening lines of the first four tercets:

The leaves on the macadam make a noise
Like tales that were told the day before yesterday,
And the wind sways like a great thing tottering,
Which suddenly is all dissolved and gone.

The second poem—that of love, of inception, of the intelligibility implicit in song—can be seen by reading in succession the latter two lines of the first four tercets, which describe the ever-recurrent appearance in nature (and in human nature) of spring, sexuality, warmth, birdsong, love, and children:

How soft the grass on which the desired
Reclines in the temperature of heaven;
Sleek in a natural nakedness,
She attends the tintinnabula
Of birds called up by more than the sun,

Birds of more wit, that substitute
Their intelligible twittering
For unintelligible thought.

The coda, declaring the overlap of the two previous poems, memorializes Stevens's daily walk to work through Hartford's Elizabeth Park, with its duck pond. Stevens takes his last look at his favorite place and sees spring:

And yet this end and this beginning are one,
And one last look at the ducks is a look
At lucent children round her in a ring.

As the poet wonders how to render not only his own unintelligible physical tottering, creative depletion, and expected dissolution but also the soft grass, the little ducklings, and the intelligible presence of a reposing Primavera, he feels that both are equally true, and must be simultaneously held in a binocular frame in which neither can obliterate or dominate the other. He is the hermit, now without a beloved, meditating in his ascetic hermitage as he slips toward death; but he does not allow himself to deny the beautiful, desirable, erotic, and fertile spring that assuages him even as he loses it. What he decides to reproduce in the style of his poem is the unintelligibility presented to us by death, which forces us to sort out the conflicting but coordinate pieces of our perceptions and thoughts. Yet even the unintelligible-when-first-read "Hermitage" reveals, stanza by stanza, a fixed pattern of recursive intelligibility when understood, reinforcing the claim for the ultimately "intelligible twittering" of the poetic mind.

A comparably strong distortion of form in the service of a binocular gaze appears in the very late poem by James Merrill called "Christmas Tree."[2]

CHRISTMAS TREE

To be
  Brought down at last
From the cold sighing mountain
Where I and the others
Had been fed, looked after, kept still,
Meant, I knew—of course I knew—
That it would be only a matter of weeks,
That there was nothing more to do.
Warmly they took me in, made much of me,
The point from the start was to keep my spirits up.
I could assent to that. For honestly,
It did help to be wound in jewels, to send
Their colors flashing forth from vents in the deep
Fragrant sable that cloaked me head to foot.
Over me then they wove a spell of shining—
Purple and silver chains, eavesdripping tinsel,
Amulets, milagros: software of silver,
A heart, a little girl, a Model T,
Two staring eyes. The angels, trumpets, BUD and BEA
(The children's names) in clownlike capitals,
Somewhere a music box whose tiny song
Played and replayed I ended before long
By loving. And in shadow behind me, a primitive IV
To keep the show going. Yes, yes, what lay ahead
Was clear: the stripping, the cold street, my chemicals
Plowed back into Earth for lives to come—
No doubt a blessing, a harvest, but one that doesn't bear,
Now or ever, dwelling upon. To have grown so thin.
Needles and bone. The little boy's hands meeting
  About my spine. The mother's voice: *Holding up wonderfully!*

No dread. No bitterness. The end beginning. Today's
    Dusk room aglow
    For the last time
    With candlelight.
    Faces love lit,
    Gifts underfoot.
Still to be so poised, so
Receptive. Still to recall, to praise.

I will return to "Christmas Tree" in the final chapter of this book, but for now I simply want to describe this as a work in the immemorial tradition of the shaped poem. It is a Christmas tree missing its left half. The forest tree is already dead, because it has previously been cut down. But in the house, it gives every appearance, with its still-green needles, of being alive and even of being more beautiful than before, feeling the warmth brought to its ornamented presence by the pleasure of the children regarding it. Merrill—already fatally ill with AIDS, but still wholly alive in spirit—invents his Christmas tree, half ghost, half evergreen, as a symbolic expression of that late binocular style which is my subject.

I hope to give perspective to these modern attempts (and others that I will take up in later chapters) by looking back at how older poets (who still imagined another world beyond this one) found a style adequate to the interface of death and life. Not all the poems I mention were written by poets at the brink of death, but they all confront the difficulty of representing, within the active horizon of life, the onset of death at that moment when, as Coleridge writes, "like strangers shelt'ring from a storm, / Hope and Despair meet in the porch of Death" ("Constancy to an Ideal Object"). How to depict that meeting within a sustained binocular view preoccupies any poet treating the supervening of death on life. We find Emily Dickinson, for instance, situating in a closed carriage the meeting of human Hope (first) and Despair (ultimately) with Death. As the poet enters, she says confidently—with, one might say, a hopeful monocular view—that the carriage contains, besides herself and her gentleman escort Death, an entity that she calls "Immortality":

> Because I could not stop for Death -
> He kindly stopped for me -
> The Carriage held but just Ourselves -
> And Immortality.

But when the carriage ultimately stops at her grave, Dickinson suspects a less certain future for herself than "Immortality," and, turning her view into a binocular one, substitutes for "Immortality" a quite different and impersonal abstract noun, "Eternity":

> Since then - 'tis Centuries - and yet
> Feels shorter than the Day
> I first surmised the Horses' Heads
> Were toward Eternity - [3]

That faceless and nameless "Eternity" is infinitely far from the hopeful personal "Immortality" promised by Dickinson's childhood Christianity; and the two abstract nouns, so similar in form and so different in meaning, face each other in a dark intellectual space, guaranteeing our realization of Dickinson's two proposals: one of individual everlasting life, and the other of featureless and blank "Eternity."

In another instance of how a binocular vision may be expressed, George Herbert (1593–1633), in "Death" (a poem to be seen more closely later), presents the riddling interface of life and death by contemplating, like Hamlet, a skull. Because to Herbert the open mouth of the living body signified song, the poet, thinking of his own death, remembers his shudder when he thought the skull mouth a hideous void:

> Death, thou wast once an uncouth hideous thing
> Nothing but bones,
> The sad effect of sadder grones:
> Thy mouth was open, but thou couldst not sing.[4]

By superimposing, as in a double exposure, the open mouth of the death's-head on the open mouth of song, Herbert forces us to see both images simultaneously.

Dickinson's and Herbert's lines represent two achievements of binocular style in pre-twentieth-century poets. Before I return to Herbert, I will consider in some detail poems by two other seventeenth-century poets, Edmund Waller (1606–87) and John Donne (1572–1631). Both set themselves the same stylistic problem: how to represent the meeting place of life and death as materially confined but conceptually limitless. Waller envisages not only the limited body, "the soul's dark cottage," but also the cosmic threshold between an old world and a celestial new one. Donne, although meeting Death in the confines of a narrow sickroom, announces that this is the moment of his grand "south-west discovery," his far Magellanic voyage through straits whose currents "yield return to none." Each poet must find a manner by which to enact the fraught nature of this moment, coordinating, in the case of Waller, both the dark cottage and the invisible threshold, and rendering credible, in the case of Donne, both the catastrophe of death and the resurrection to come.

I begin with Waller's infinitely touching poem "Of the Last Verses in the Book." The poet tells us that he has become blind and can no longer read or write. But before he drops his pen, he writes out his "last verses," composed less by the mortal body (with its unruly passions) than by the unbodied soul (who is, as *anima*, female). Weighing his present painful physical blindness against a past mental blindness to heavenly realities, Waller shows stoic resolve:

> When we for Age could neither read nor write,
> The Subject made us able to indite.
> The Soul, with Nobler Resolutions deckt,
> The Body stooping, does Herself erect:
> No Mortal Parts are requisite to raise
> Her, that Unbody'd can her Maker praise.
> The Seas are quiet, when the Winds give o'er,
> So calm are we, when Passions are no more:
> For then we know how vain it was to boast
> Of fleeting Things, so certain to be lost.
> Clouds of Affection from our younger Eyes
> Conceal that emptiness, which Age descries.
> The Soul's dark Cottage, batter'd and decay'd,
> Lets in new Light thrô chinks that time has made;
> Stronger by weakness, wiser Men become
> As they draw near to their Eternal home:
> Leaving the Old, both Worlds at once they view,
> That stand upon the Threshold of the New.
> —*Miratur Limen Olympi*, Virgil[5]

Because Waller, remembering the Virgilian threshold of Olympus, is convinced that "The Soul's dark Cottage . . . / Lets in new Light thrô chinks that time has made," he needs to make real to us both bodily darkness and spiritual light. His first sestet conveys the physical darkness: we hear that the poet can neither read nor write, and that his body is stooping. By the second sestet, the great initial effort required to erect the soul and "indite" under the condition of blindness has subsided into a reflection on the calming of the passions. There is no compensatory light as yet, but the poet has begun to reconsider his present blindness—was he not more blind earlier in life, when passion's "clouds of affection" concealed from his eyes the emptiness of worldly "fleeting things"? By the third sestet, a sustaining spiritual illumination arrives, not through the eyes but—in an arresting and poignant metaphor—through the very wounds suffered by the "batter'd and decay'd" body. (The adjectives illustrate the double plight of trauma and age.) Successively opened "chinks" take over the function of the lost eyes, and the rays of a hitherto unknown light are thereby enabled, through trauma, to penetrate the "dark cottage" of mortality. As the soul prepares to cross the threshold dividing earth from heaven, her illumination gradually increases until, paradoxically stronger in weakness and wiser in blindness, she sees herself approaching the source of light, a whole new world.

Or so it would be if the poem had been written in the first-person singular. But we perceive that Waller has begun in the first-person plural (extending his poem to all of us in our last days) and that he has, unexpectedly, spoken of his soul and his body in third-person abstraction—"the Soul," "the Body"—as though he were already beginning to detach himself from them as they prepare to detach themselves from one another. By the time of the third stanza, all reference is voiced in the third-person plural: "men" become stronger and wiser, and "they" view two worlds at once. Waller cannot as yet join such men on the preparatory threshold of death; he is still alive. But he is old enough, and blind enough, to say, in the present tense of old age, that men become, by their newly admitted spiritual light, stronger and wiser as they "draw near to their Eternal home." Nothing any longer is "fleeting"—all worldly attractions have fled for good. The effect of balance in the last two lines, as the poet imagines a momentary pause on the journey "home," depends on his creating for us, by means of style, that threshold on which the soul will stand. The main affirmation of the close—"both Worlds at once they view"—is poised evenly between "Leaving the Old" and "the Threshold of the New," while the "old" of departure becomes incorporated into the "threshold" of anticipation. And in this truly binocular vision, the freestanding adjective "New," closing the poem and predicated of the celestial World, is ratified by its echo of the earlier phrase "new Light," which evoked the soul's first glimpse, within its "dark Cottage," of the rays of heaven.

Wallace Stevens's elegy for George Santayana, "To an Old Philosopher in Rome," enables us to see Waller's poem resonating, but changed, within modern writing. Stevens borrows Waller's Virgilian image of the "threshold" for the interface of life and death. But Stevens cannot echo Waller's confidence in a "new World" beyond that threshold and must create a different binocular view of Santayana's death and life. Stevens begins in Waller's vein, speaking of Santayana, still alive in Rome, as being poised "on the threshold of heaven," but the modern poet conceives heaven in a secular fashion—as the full realization, in time, of what we have seen, desired, and created in life. Stevens asserts that "the threshold, Rome, and that more merciful Rome / Beyond" are "alike in the make of the mind":

> It is as if in a human dignity
> Two parallels become one, a perspective, of which
> Men are part both in the inch and in the mile.

Santayana, Stevens continues, is "a citizen of heaven though still of Rome." At the moment of death, it is Santayana's lifelong creation, his edifice of thought, that becomes, in Stevens's view, a final architecture of "total grandeur at the end." Santayana, through his philosophical imagination, inhabits the "total grandeur of a total edifice":

> Total grandeur of a total edifice,
> Chosen by an inquisitor of structures
> For himself. He stops upon this threshold,
> As if the design of all his words takes form
> And frame from thinking and is realized.

If we try to think of an alternative way in which Waller might have imagined his last days, we could conceive of his staging "Of the Last Verses" as a gradual and fulfilling chronological pilgrimage during which the soul, at first full of youthful passions, journeys downward into the sadness and blindness of age until, facing the threshold of eternity, it becomes aware that its suffering has enabled it to see celestial light and, at the end, the new World from which the light issues. But that linear teleological advance would have minimized the poet's actual state at the time of writing—he is stooping, blind, afflicted, inhabiting a "batter'd cottage." We are eventually permitted to feel the vitality-within-decay of the new light, made so physically real by the painful "chinks" through which it penetrates, but at the same time we encounter, even on the threshold of eternal light, the weak and hampered state of the poet's body. Waller sums up his binocular view in the phrase "stronger by weakness," which by its paradoxical style asserts the inextricability, at the interface of life and death, of bodily failure and spiritual strength. Stevens, too, for all the grandeur he ascribes to Santayana, makes us feel the body's decline as he pleads with Santayana to articulate for us the nature of modern death. Like Waller, Stevens imagines a paradoxical grandeur found only in misery and ruin. Addressing Santayana, Stevens describes him as

> Impatient for the grandeur that you need
>
> In so much misery; and yet finding it
> Only in misery, the afflatus of ruin,
> Profound poetry of the poor and of the dead.

Other convincing transmutations of Christian elegy by modern poets will appear later in this book. But now I turn back from Stevens's echoing of Waller's threshold and the pain preceding it to my second example of the style of Christian poets who delineate the state of living in the face of death while expecting a future in heaven. John Donne's self-elegy "A Hymn to God My God, in My Sickness" reveals that Donne, terrified at the actuality of death, adopts as his first strategy an attempt to deny as much as possible a truly binocular view, emphasizing instead a stereoscopic assimilation of the fearful unknown reaches of death to the known dimensions of life. The poet's sickroom becomes, by this will to similarity, an antechamber to God's holy room; his present music is, he says, the same as the music he will play, or become, in heaven; and what he here enacts in thought, he will in heaven carry out in action. His assimilations then become geographical ones: by comparing his body to a flat map, he makes his West his East, his death his resurrection, and his journey to the afterlife a project comparable to the earthly journeys of famous travelers, from Magellan to Marco Polo. Even when Donne turns away from these witty coercive analogies to engage in direct prayer, he is intent on a form of metaphorical religious assimilation, conflating the place of joy (Paradise) with the place of pain (Calvary), metamorphosing one crown (Christ's crown of thorns) into another (his own crown of salvation), assuring himself that one bodily fluid (the sweat of Adam's brow, reproduced by his own fever) will be redeemed by another such fluid (Christ's blood). In

Donne's final assimilation of there to here, he makes himself—
the famous preacher of sermons in Saint Paul's—both the of-
ficiant at his own funeral and the audience to his own consola-
tory but minatory sermon.

Donne's palpable stylistic effort to fuse into a single image
each set of opposite states is made in the interest of obscuring
the enormous difference between sickroom and God's room,
death and eternal life, earthly journeys and spiritual ones,
preaching in public and praying on one's deathbed. (In the
event, Donne recovered from the sickness that precipitated
"Hymne to God my God, in my sicknesse"; nevertheless, the
poem arises from his conviction that he is in the last moments
of life, about to enter the precincts of death.) Here is this conspicuously assimilative poem, whose strategy of denial of difference breaks down only in its closing line:

HYMNE TO GOD MY GOD, IN MY SICKNESSE

Since I am comming to that Holy roome,
　　　Where, with thy Quire of Saints for evermore,
I shall be made thy Musique; As I come
　　　I tune the Instrument here at the dore,
　　　And what I must doe then, thinke here before.

Whilst my Physitians by their love are growne
　　　Cosmographers, and I their Mapp, who lie
Flat on this bed, that by them may be showne
　　　That this is my South-west discoverie
　　　Per fretum febris, by these straits to die,

I joy, that in these straits, I see my West;
　　　For, though theire currants yeeld returne to none,
What shall my West hurt me? As West and East
　　　In all flatt Maps (and I am one) are one,
　　　So death doth touch the Resurrection.

Is the Pacifique Sea my home? Or are
   The Easterne riches? Is *Jerusalem?*
Anyan, and *Magellan,* and *Gibraltare,*
    All straits, and none but straits are wayes to them,
    Whether where *Japhet* dwelt, or *Cham,* or *Sem.*

We thinke that *Paradise* and *Calvarie,*
   Christs Crosse, and *Adams* tree, stood in one place;
Looke Lord, and finde both *Adams* met in me;
    As the first *Adams* sweat surrounds my face,
    May the last *Adams* blood my soule embrace.

So, in his purple wrapp'd receive mee Lord,
   By these his thornes give me his other Crowne;
And as to others soules I preach'd thy word,
    Be this my Text, my Sermon to mine owne,
    Therefore that he may raise the Lord throws down.[6]

After all the insistent assimilating of the unknown future
side of the interface, that of death, to the known present side,
that of life, the final text of Donne's sermon to himself comes
as a shock. In it he sharply distinguishes—for the first time in
the poem—the two sides of the interface, now admitting that
being thrown down into death must precede being raised into
immortality. He borrows here from Psalm 102:9–10, in which
the psalmist contrasts his former state—being lifted up by
God—with his present one, in which he has been cast down:

For I have eaten ashes like bread,
   and mingled my drink with weeping,
Because of thine indignation and thy wrath;
   for thou has lifted me up, and cast me down.

Donne reverses the psalmist's order: he is now cast down and
wants God to raise him up. He still retains, at the end, a trace

of his former will to assimilation; he links the two opposite states by making "raise" the intended effect of "throws down" and by ascribing both equally to God's agency. The crucial final-line "text" of Donne's self-sermon gains additional significance not only by its scriptural source and epigrammatic closing function but also by its rhetorical difference—as a direct-address homily to the poet's own soul—from the speech act of prayer to God, which otherwise organizes the whole hymn.

The striking isolation of this final line leads us to a backward glance at the rhyme scheme (ababb) of Donne's stanza. Given its rhymes, the stanza "ought" to end after its fourth line, when its rhyme is "completed," abab. In stanzas 1, 2, and 4, confirming such an intuition, the fifth line is syntactically supplementary rather than essential; in stanzas 3 and 5, however, the fifth line is necessary to the sense and thereby justifies its existence. But the closing line of the final stanza, although essential, is a cited text rather than a personal narration. The personal supplicatory voice of the dying Donne, insisting on his imaginative conflation of unknown death and known life, has disappeared, vanquished by the undeniable Pauline axiom that whom the Lord loveth, he chasteneth; whom he wishes to raise, he throws down. There is, then, no seamless and facile assimilative passage, as the poet had hoped, from life to death. Donne struggles so hard against the actual binocular vision that would admit cleanly the two distinct aspects, mortal and immortal, of the last look, that his final collapse into an admission of the utter duality between affliction and resurrection sets into distinct stylistic relief his earlier determination to make the afterlife appear a smooth analogue to living.

We have seen that in "Hymne to God my God, in my sicknesse," Donne has employed a form of palimpsest (a new text

16

written over a former incompletely erased one), consistently easing the fear of death by superimposing a "heavenly" image ("God's holy room") on an actual earthly one (the sickroom), the East of resurrection over the West of mortal illness. In Donne's other great poem of death, "A Hymne to God the Father," we find that the figure blurring the sharp interface of continuing life and imminent death is again that of the palimpsest. This time, however, it is a figure not of images but of words, in which a single word or phrase is reinscribed over itself. Each of the three six-line stanzas of the "Hymne" is generated by the reiterated words "done" and "more," and the first two stanzas begin "Wilt thou forgive that sin . . . ?" By this repetition we are made to realize that all the stanzas are variants of a single underlying template, that of confession, with Donne as the penitent and God as the confessor. The penitent rehearses, in the course of the poem, several varieties of sin—"that sin where I begun," "that sin, through which I run," "that sin by which I have won / Others to sin," and "that sin which I did shun"—all of them singularly unspecified, as though God were already aware of the particulars of Donne's former faults that have generated these vague categories. Here are Donne's first two stanzas, reinscribing "Wilt thou forgive that sin" and inaugurating the immobile rhymes that create the superposition of successive sins, past and present:

I.

Wilt thou forgive that sinne where I begunne,
    Which is my sin, though it were done before?
Wilt thou forgive that sinne, through which I runne,
    And do run still: though still I do deplore?
        When thou hast done, thou hast not done,
            For, I have more.

II.

Wilt thou forgive that sinne by which I have wonne
    Others to sinne? and, made my sinne their doore?
Wilt thou forgive that sinne which I did shunne
    A yeare, or two: but wallowed in, a score?
        When thou hast done, thou hast not done,
          For I have more.

The third version inscribed on the template of confession will end the poem, which until this point has been playing with five tenses: the future ("Wilt thou forgive"); the present ("which is my sin"); the present perfect ("by which I have won"); the imperfect ("wallowed in a score"); and the future perfect ("When thou hast done"—the equivalent of "when you will have forgiven all those"). By phrasing the future perfect as though it were the present perfect ("When thou hast done"), Donne suspends his poem in an uncertain moment—that of a hoped-for future represented as though it has already happened.

Because the third version of the confession must maintain the unswerving template rhymes on "done" and "more," it must resemble its predecessors; but since it has to resolve the poem, it must differ from them. In the closing stanza, Donne for the first time makes a confession in which he specifies his sin: "I have a sin of fear." And for the first time he envisages a future not God's ("Wilt thou forgive") but his own—a future of damnation where he may "perish on the shore." Because he has—with the word "perish"—at last admitted the abyss separating death from life, he can banish all his tense-splitting and look to a different model of hope, not that of tensed time but that of the untensed eternity of the resplendent son of God:

III.

I have a sinne of feare, that when I have spunne
    My last thred, I shall perish on the shore;

> But sweare by thy selfe, that at my death thy sonne
> Shall shine as he shines now, and heretofore;
> And, having done that, Thou haste done,
> I feare no more.

Donne has resolved his earlier uneasy slippage among tenses by directing his last look at the perpetual presence of the Son/Sun, who "shall shine" (at the death to come) as he "shines now" (in the poet's present) and as he shone "heretofore" (in the past). The poet's death, in consequence, is no longer envisaged within a temporal continuum of uncertain hope or terrified fear, but is absorbed within the timelessness of providential redemption. Through his emphasis on tenses, Donne demonstrates stylistically the anxiety which seeks to obscure the distinction between death and life; that anxiety flitters between the present, the recent past, the continuous past, the ancestral past (evoked by "heretofore"), the future, and the future perfect. Anxious ourselves under the flurry of Donne's constantly changing tenses, we are relieved when Donne turns his gaze from time to eternity, at last making God's sworn "done" match the fate of "Donne." The normal human resistance to contemplating the unimaginable fissure between life and death generates, in Donne's aggressively visible manner, the manufacture of a confusing multiplicity of times until, in the third stanza, the poet can, by finally admitting the danger of perishing on death's "shore," forsake body-time in favor of soul-time and end his poem.

George Herbert could not be more different from Donne in the strategy he adopts when depicting the encounter of life and death. While Donne strove to allay anxiety by assimilating one state to the other, Herbert, in "Death," is so deeply intent on drawing the ghastly contrast between life and death that he at first exhibits unconcealed revulsion as he brings his skeletal Death-figure into view. As we have seen, the skull, open-mouthed, cannot sing; open-socketed, it can shed no tears; after some years in the grave, the flesh that had clothed the skeleton has turned to dust; and the bones of the corpse have degenerated into mere sticks. Artists' paintings and woodcuts of skeletons in the Dance of Death lie behind Herbert's grim *vanitas* of the mortal bodies of his companions in life; as for the winged souls of the poet's dead, they have departed from their earthly nest, leaving behind only the empty and lifeless shells from which they have flown. The purely naturalistic look at Death in the first half of Herbert's poem is "uncontaminated" by any consolation except the past tense in which it is voiced; the souls of the dead, says the poet, have vanished into invisibility, and graveside mourners confront only their dust, which extorts tears.

Herbert presents this opening naturalistic last look as a temporally mistaken one, but he does not yet tell us how to correct it:

> Death, thou wast once an uncouth hideous thing,
>> Nothing but bones,
>> The sad effect of sadder grones:
> Thy mouth was open, but thou couldst not sing.
>
> For we consider'd thee as at some six
>> Or ten yeares hence,
>> After the losse of life and sense,
> Flesh being turn'd to dust, and bones to sticks.
>
> We lookt on this side of thee, shooting short;
>> Where we did finde
>> The shells of fledge souls left behinde,
> Dry dust, which sheds no tears, but may extort.

"We lookt on this side of thee, shooting short," explains the poet; what would it be to shoot the arrows of sight farther, so as to gain a view of the other side of the body's encounter with Death? What can Herbert do in the second half of his poem to be "fair" to Death and make it seem less "uncouth"? In his effort to reclaim Death from hideousness, must he erase its connection with bones and dust? Can he console himself—as many less talented Christian poets have done—by obliterating the decay of the mortal body in favor of the glory of the immortal soul in heaven?

We find that Herbert does not ignore our natural attachment to the body robbed from us by Death. Instead (he says reassuringly), since we are enabled by the death of Christ to look through dying rather than at it, we can view in prospect our natural bodies at the Last Judgment, when, in glorified form, wearing their "new array," they will have rejoined our waiting souls. Herbert can then address Death in new terms: no longer aesthetically repellent, it has become "full of grace," attractive, something sought after:

> But since our Saviours death did put some bloud
> > Into thy face;
> > Thou art grown fair and full of grace,
> Much in request, much sought for, as a good.
>
> For we do now behold thee gay and glad,
> > As at dooms-day;
> > When souls shall wear their new array,
> And all thy bones with beautie shall be clad.
>
> Therefore we can go die as sleep, and trust
> > Half that we have
> > Unto an honest faithfull grave;
> Making our pillows either down, or dust.

At Herbert's doomsday, our past as bones is not erased; nor do we now, even when reminded of our glorious eventual destiny, forget our present potential to become dust at any moment. But the joyful change of attitude brought about by "our Saviours death" (as the ambience of Herbert's poem alters from a materialistic view of the skeleton to a Christian one) has to be made real, stylistically, in the bald light of what we already know from looking directly at the grave's "hideous" bones. Death has undergone the sort of magical transformation into a human figure that is familiar in folktale and legend. The congratulatory air of Herbert's fourth and fifth stanzas has the poet's usual touch of comedy-in-seriousness: Death is at present a celebrity much in request, newly adorned by the poet with alliterative phrases drawn from the lexicon of legend— "fair and full of grace," "gay and glad." The little joke of Death's social rehabilitation can then be laid aside for the earnest future-tense doomsday vision, as newly arrayed souls rejoice, clad no longer in a mortal garment, as in the past, but in an eternal "beautie," which by alliterating with "bloud" (of Jesus) and "bones" (of the dead) connects forever the aesthetic, the redemptive, and the mortal. It would be a different matter entirely had Herbert forsaken the bones for something else: ["When souls shall wear their new array, / And in their glory be by beautie clad."][7] No: Herbert is not so much describing doomsday as speaking to the very concept of Death; not "their" bones but "thy" bones. Even the bony skeletal form takes on imputed radiance when Death is seen as our necessary conveyor to an aesthetically superior body.

As he draws his gentle closing moral, Herbert drops the address to Death in order to speak to and for us. We need not fear the sudden death that comes like a thief in the night; it would only hasten the day when we receive our transfigured body. The body, which is the only thing Death can touch, is only half of us; the other half, the soul, is immortal. The grave is only another bed, where our body will sleep until doomsday. In the certain faith of redemption, Herbert says, we can go to sleep or to death with equal trust. But Herbert, while affirming this faith, does not deny the chilling character of the posthumous interim of decay: if we sleep on a down pillow in our bed, we must sleep on a pillow of dust in the grave. By ending his poem on the word "dust," Herbert is faithful to his first, naturalistic, look at Death; but by rhyming "dust" with "trust," as he at last looks through Death, Herbert recapitulates his entire argument for a new view of Death. By alliterating "down" and "dust," Herbert suggests how easily "we can go die as sleep." The grave is "honest" and "faithfull" because it is charged with rendering back, on the Last Day, every grain of dust that it contains: it is a good and faithful servant.

The satisfying conclusiveness of the ending of "Death" depends on Herbert's efforts to transcribe fairly both the human last look at, and the Christian last look through, Death, as he depicts, in his binocular style, the hideous beside the glorious, conjoining his original pity for ugly Death with the subsequent admiring of him once he is beautified by Christ's sacrifice. Herbert's fastidiousness and aesthetic intensity recoiled from the sight of the charnel house of Death; his Christian convictions granted him (to use Wordsworth's words) "the faith that looks through death"; but only his personal kindness invented the little fable that lets Death be new clad in a garment suitable for the celestial wedding feast. "Our Saviour" has saved hideous Death, as well as sinful mankind. Even a non-Christian can relish Herbert's tender effort to rehabilitate Death and can understand why, for an aesthete, Doomsday must regenerate everything, even Death itself, in an achieved beauty.

As we recall the older poems' efforts to be just to the interface of death and life, to create a genuinely binocular last look, we have seen that Waller's poem "Of the Last Verses in the Book," although it draws nearer to illumination as it progresses, succeeds in retaining the "old" battered and decayed body even on the very threshold of the new world. And while both of Donne's two "Hymns" make an aggrieved effort to refuse the fearful nature of dying by assimilating it to living, that self-deceiving effort collapses, not only in the poet's self-sermon admitting the distinct difference between being painfully thrown down and being gloriously raised, but also in the abolition of shifting human tenses in favor of Donne's acknowledgment of the Son's tenseless eternity. Each of these stylistic choices attempts in the end to be accurate and even-handed in its last look: so much for life, so much for death. But in these Christian poems of faith, the balance is necessarily tipped, as we see, against death.

On the other hand, in "The Hermitage at the Center" and "Christmas Tree" we have glimpsed what may happen when the concept of an afterlife is no longer available to poets taking the last look. As we consider poems from the last books of Stevens, Plath, Lowell, Bishop, and Merrill, we will see them striving to do justice to difficult truths through stylistic means. Weighing fairly what it means to be alive but mortal, they hope to find a manner that can take in, in a single steady gaze, life and death. Stevens's looks at the worst; Plath's struggle between melodrama and restraint; Lowell's account of death as a set of successive subtractions from an always vital existence; Bishop's oscillations between being caught in the body and being freed into expression; and Merrill's resort to a renewed naïveté before the indescribable future will all appear as heartfelt stylistic responses to a creative predicament faced by poets unable to assume an afterlife.

2

Looking at the Worst: Wallace Stevens's *The Rock*

Wallace Stevens had always refused to yield to Alfred Knopf's desire for a *Collected Poems*; such a volume, Stevens must have felt, would impose a premature closure on his writing life. But finally, after completing a group of new poems—to be called *The Rock*—and fearing (with reason) that he would not live to write another book, Stevens allowed the publication of his *Collected Poems*, which appeared (by Alfred Knopf's decision) on Stevens's seventy-fifth birthday, October 2, 1954. Ten months later, Stevens died of advanced stomach cancer. During the five years preceding his death, as we can see from some of his late letters, his energy diminished and his senses became less responsive; even the coming of spring, which would always lift his spirits, was no longer a sovereign remedy. "At my ripe age," he wrote to his friend Barbara Church in April 1950, "the world begins to seem a little thin . . . This year the coming of spring has left me cold."[1] He was struck by "the occasionally frightening aspect of the past, into which so many that we have known have disappeared, almost as if they had never been real" (*L* 954). After an operation disclosed terminal cancer, Stevens admitted, in the month before his death, "There is no chance, I think, of any new poems. Most of the time when I am at home, I drowse" (*L* 955). There are in *The Rock* many poems representing and enacting the interface of life and death, but here I will also mention, for completeness of description, some late uncollected poems as well as two poems preceding *The Rock*.

Stevens was a lawyer, and often, in a poem, he took a stance of formal argument, advancing, aspect by aspect, through his topic. His commitment to a poetry of "accuracy with respect to the structure of reality" demanded that he analyze that structure or blueprint, both as it appeared at the moment of writing and as it had changed for him over time. He was never one for a literal transcription of an event or occasion, but he had an unequaled sense of the architectonics of thought and imagination. To express the structures of being with accuracy demanded that he invent poetic structures and styles adequate to them.

In *The Rock* and in poems written too late for the *Collected Poems*, Stevens examined three chief premises about the last phase of being, when life faces death. The first two premises—that age is a paralytic stasis of the body and mind alike and that death is a biological horror—caused him anguish. His third premise, however, is that mortality confers a compensatory value on life. Stasis, horror, and an honoring of life even in the face of death: I will take up all three premises, considering the different emotional pressures exerted on Stevens by each premise, and the poet's consequent imaginative inventions of structure and style.

In his most acquiescent mood, Stevens was instructed in his feelings about death by overhearing the last soliloquy of his muse, his interior paramour, who says to him:

> Light the first light of evening, as in a room
> In which we rest and, for small reason, think
> The world imagined is the ultimate good.

We can understand why Stevens, sitting in evening solitude in a narrow upstairs room in Hartford, composing in his mind the poems that he would soon write, invented an inner muse that would reassure him of the supreme value of that "intensest rendezvous" between poet and paramour-muse. But when Stevens spoke of late life in his own voice, he often produced an altogether bleaker tone. The structure of reality, in the approach of death, sometimes seemed to him a wholly entropic one, about to come to a halt in a stasis that would be final. This premise produced a problem of representation: how can a poem allow itself to evolve dynamically as a future-oriented structure (as it always must) if its thematic duty is to enact stasis? The famous poem "The Plain Sense of Things," in spite of its familiarity, has to be quoted here because it is the *ars poetica* of the poetry of stasis, replicating irreversible ruin.

The story preceding "The Plain Sense of Things" (deducible from this poem and others) would go as follows: "Once upon a time there was a great house inhabited by a turbaned ruler, an effendi; in the garden there was a great pond, pink with water lilies, next to which the effendi had in the past sat with his beloved; a greenhouse supplied the house with flowers; a chimney showed by its plume of smoke the warmth of the foyer inside.[2] But now all warmth has left the house, and the speaker forces himself to make an inventory of the waste land that surrounds him, even while asking himself why he should be compelled to undertake such a mournful task. Energy has departed: the house has declined, the leaves have fallen, the pond is muddied, the lilies are dead, silence pervades the landscape, and the human speaker himself feels inanimate and inert."

In the opening view of the poem, stasis has arrived and appears unchangeable. But the poem arrives—as a poem of stasis "should" not—at a surprising change of view, in which the poet steels himself to a new orientation. At the impasse of an ending, a terminal death-recognition (of fear, of fury, of failure) is met with an evolving life-resolution (to see, to learn, to know). First, the poet, using the generalizing "we" instead of the revealing "I," admits the collapse—after a fantastic effort—of a life's endeavor and (perhaps recalling Shakespeare and Keats) acknowledges the carrion flies attending that collapse.³ When a stoic will to knowledge of the new state arises, some stylistic means must be found to link mourning recognition to stern resolve, since they occur within the same sensibility. Almost unwillingly, and surprisingly, Stevens concedes that his present unchanging and wintry state is not new but *old*. Before he possessed the house, the beloved, the pond, he actually inhabited a similar waste land. He is now returning to, not arriving at, "a plain sense of things":

> After the leaves have fallen, we return
> To a plain sense of things. It is as if
> We had come to an end of the imagination,
> Inanimate in an inert savoir.
>
> It is difficult even to choose the adjective
> For this blank cold, this sadness without cause.
> The great structure has become a minor house.
> No turban walks across the lessened floors.

By mentioning the difficulty of choosing a suitable adjective for his scene, Stevens reminds us of the way the adjective had served him in the more affluent past—as enhancement, as incandescence, as "the amorous adjective aflame" ("The Man with the Blue Guitar"). Now Stevens forces us to note the adjectives he tries out: "blank," "minor," "lessened." But to decorate the scene with adjectives at all, he knows, is to falsify its utter emotional emptiness. He will extirpate adjectives and station himself (except for the hyperbolic adjective "fantastic") in unadorned fact:

> The greenhouse never so badly needed paint.
> The chimney is fifty years old and slants to one side.
> A fantastic effort has failed, a repetition
> In a repetitiousness of men and flies.

What style is adequate to this state of affairs? The formal linguistic equivalent of emotional stasis is repetition—of phonemes, of words, of syntactic forms such as phrases in apposition, or even of larger utterances. We first see the repetition-enacting stasis in the immobile phonemes of the line "In-an-im-ate in an in-ert savoir." Repetition continues through the figure of apposition: "this blank cold, this sadness without cause." The subsequent details of decline are imprisoned in a repetitive syntax: four one-line sentences, beginning with "The greenhouse," repeat the same rigid subject-predicate formulation. Finally the poem emphasizes its own technique of stasis, asserting the tautological presence of "a repetition / In a repetitiousness."

We now encounter the characteristic Stevensian "yet" of second thoughts, asserting a determination to counter the stasis of permanent depletion. But that "yet" is not permitted to repudiate what the eye has seen, cannot artificially urge the stasis into a false renewal, and cannot invoke, as a Christian writer might, the promise of a better life to be. If the repetitiveness of end-game stasis cannot be evaded, how, then, can the dynamic and yet stoic Stevensian "yet" be made stylistically convincing? The short answer is that Stevens replaces his earlier "inanimate" and "inert" quailing in repetitive paralysis by rephrasing the end stage as a phase of enlightenment. His stance resembles, in this respect, Waller's acknowledgment of "new light" entering the self through the wounds of age and damage. Can Stevens, while prolonging the repetitive linguistic marks of stasis, invent a stylistic force representing new knowledge? And since the mark of stasis is the impossibility of the exhausted soul's finding a mode of utterance, what can substitute for utterance as a counterweight to the oppressed silence that has replaced voice? Stevens draws himself up to a final view of the structure of reality as it appears when his leaves of pages no longer speak. Although his imagination once found its reflection in nature's mirror, now the formerly mirroring pond has "water like dirty glass." He can no longer see through a glass, even if darkly: what will happen when he comes face to face with absence and silence?

> Yet the absence of the imagination had
> Itself to be imagined. The great pond,
> The plain sense of it, without reflections, leaves,
> Mud, water like dirty glass, expressing silence
>
> Of a sort, silence of a rat come out to see,
> The great pond and its waste of the lilies, all this
> Had to be imagined as an inevitable knowledge,
> Required, as a necessity requires.

The decision to insert a non-human view—in the moment when a rat, the posthumous seeing eye of the poem, succeeds the carrion flies—enables this strangely consoling rendition of a poet's final silence. The effort to maintain the activity of cognition, even though everything physical has come to a halt, produces the wonderful and unpredictable rat. The "great structure" may have declined into a "minor house," but the "great pond" is, the poet concedes, still "the great pond," its expanse unaffected even though its lilies have wasted, are waste. The plain sense of things continues to generate its characteristic static repetitions: of "imagination" in "the absence of the imagination / Had itself to be imagined"; of "silence" in "silence / Of a sort, silence of a rat"; of "require" in "required, as a necessity requires." After all this stasis of dogged repetition, the final triumph of the poem is its finding what it had been seeking, "the adjective for this blank cold," a discovery the poet had earlier thought difficult, perhaps even impossible. Once he arrives at the adjective he has been looking for—the adjective "*in*-evita-ble" in the penultimate line of the poem—we feel it has all along been hovering in the wings, waiting to contradict "*In*-an-imate *in* an *in*-ert savoir." The last line—with its repetition of the Latin for "seeking again and again," *re-quaerere*, "Required . . . requires"—ends (as it must) by reiterating the factual life-stasis with which the poem began. But within that immutabil-ity of paralyzed external circumstance, a repeated activity of inquiry into "inevitable knowledge" keeps the previously inert imagination alive, keeps it "coming out to see," to take its last looks, even if only to gaze upon its own displayed absence, and to live, beside the "great pond," in its own sad silence.

"The Plain Sense of Things" is a post-elegiac poem. Every-thing one cared about is already gone, and in that moment we are suddenly aware that there had existed, earlier in life, a com-parable blank moment before we encountered our loved places, people, and possessions. Externally, then, there is a return to that earlier blankness; but internally we experience, in compar-ing the blanknesses, not a simple acquiescent return to a for-mer uninvestigated desolate condition but rather our need to name and enumerate our losses—and then to pose the re-quired and inevitable query, seeking and acquiring a new knowledge of deprivation.

We must go back for a moment to the elegies that preceded *The Rock* to understand how fully Stevens understood a dynami-cally evolving kind of elegy before going beyond it to the stasis of "The Plain Sense of Things" on the one hand, and to the hor-ror of "Madame La Fleurie" on the other. The most naked of Stevens's earlier elegies is the one mourning his dead parents and his estranged wife. Realizing that such deaths and frustra-tions are common and occur in every life, he grimly entitles his familial elegy "World without Peculiarity." I quote the hopeless beginning, with its recital of individual losses, each followed by an outcry of protest and pain:

> The day is great and strong—
> But his father was strong, that lies now
> In the poverty of dirt.
>
> Nothing could be more hushed than the way
> The moon moves toward the night.
> But what his mother was returns and cries on his breast.
>
> The red ripeness of round leaves is thick
> With the spices of red summer.
> But she that he loved turns cold at his light touch.
>
> What good is it that the earth is justified,
> That it is complete, that it is an end,
> That in itself it is enough?

After this outburst of increasing sadness, the lament ends, not wholly successfully, with the poet attempting to believe that his losses can eventually be absorbed within nature.

In another grief-saturated elegy, "Burghers of Petty Death" (concerning, I would guess, the grave of his parents),[4] Stevens reports, and reproduces, the entire unimportance to the universe of any particular deaths. His parents, of Pennsylvania Dutch stock, are anonymous "burghers" buried in the cemetery that received their "petty death":

> These two by the stone wall
> Are a slight part of death.
> The grass is still green.
>
> But there is a total death,
> A devastation, a death of great height

And depth, covering all surfaces,
Filling the mind.

These are the small townsmen of death,
A man and a woman, like two leaves
That keep clinging to a tree
Before winter freezes and grows black—

Of great height and depth
Without any feeling, an imperium of quiet,
In which a wasted figure, with an instrument,
Propounds blank final music.

Of course to a bereft son the death of his parents is of enormous consequence. In an attempt to give equal credence to the cruel fact of cosmic indifference to death and the disabling fact of filial sorrow, Stevens (as we saw him doing in "The Hermitage at the Center") writes two poems within one: the poem in which the petty deaths are of no great weight, and the poem in which the "wasted figure" of the son wordlessly, in "an imperium of quiet," plays by the grave a blank and final music. An impersonal and indifferent voice speaks the "left" half of the poem, while a narrator who can read the mind of the devastated son, and can contest the indifference expressed on the left, speaks the "right" half.

INDIFFERENCE	GRIEF
These two by the stone wall	
Are a slight part of death.	
The grass is still green.	
	But there is a total death,
	A devastation, a death of great
	height,
	And depth, covering all
	surfaces,
	Filling the mind.

These are the small townsmen of death,
A man and a woman,

        like two leaves
        That keep clinging to a tree,

Before winter freezes and
grows black—

        Of great height and depth

Without any feeling, an
imperium of quiet,

        In which a wasted figure, with
        an instrument,
        Propounds blank final music.

As this arrangement makes evident, by the middle of "Burghers of Petty Death" the two "poems" are impossible to keep separate. The pathos of the couple's last moments as they cling to life has been projected by the son onto the entire world, "covering all surfaces." As the son repeats, in the fourth stanza, his early words describing his individual measure of those deaths, "Of great height and depth," the grief that was previously inside his consciousness, "filling the mind," is externalized into the "blank final music" of an elegy infiltrated by the chill of nature's view. Stevens's forensic debate, setting nature's freezing indifference to human extinction against the filial shock of "total death," creates an accuracy with respect to that emotional structure of reality in which the unimportance of death to the universe, and the importance of parental death to the son, are at almost complete odds. Stevens's last look at personal relations against the stasis of the grave grants both the monumental significance of those relations to the filial mind and their meaninglessness in the natural world. In this binocular vision, the poem's impersonal look at the passage of the seasons from green grass to black cold counters the grieving filial look at the pathos of the "clinging" couple.

The Rock and the poems written between that collection and Stevens's death relentlessly expose the contrast between Stevens's earlier poems of pathos elegizing others, and the later and harsher poems elegizing himself. The poet in "Burghers of Petty Death" could create, with an instrument, a "blank final music" for his parents, but in the November of his own life, the music of death, although loudly and deeply present, is inaccessible to consciousness, feeling, instrumentation, and language. The speaker's mental space is a November-like region. Only the North Wind, for the moment, can transmit the music of death as it passes through the trees, and the powerful but nonverbal North Wind, withholding its revelation, seems to Stevens "like a critic of God, the world // And human nature," enthroned in an alien, non-human, undomesticated wilderness. The North Wind is a person; he sits in "his own" wilderness and is not available to the human world. Once more, Stevens depicts, by repetition, stasis as the only structure of reality now visible and audible. Here is "The Region November":

> It is hard to hear the north wind again,
> And to watch the treetops, as they sway.
>
> They sway, deeply and loudly, in an effort,
> So much less than feeling, so much less than speech,
>
> Saying and saying, the way things say
> On the level of that which is not yet knowledge:
>
> A revelation not yet intended.
> It is like a critic of God, the world
>
> And human nature, pensively seated
> On the waste throne of his own wilderness.
>
> Deeplier, deeplier, loudlier, loudlier,
> The trees are swaying, swaying, swaying.

The repetitions exemplifying this stasis include five in-stances (including variants) of "sway," three of "deep," three of "loud," three of "say," two of "so much less," and two of "not yet." The poem seems unable to gain access to what the trees are "saying and saying" as they are "swaying, swaying, swaying": if only the poet could delete their "w's" (so to speak), he could interpret their motion as something said. Unable to decipher any meaning, he falls back on his only support, language, think-ing that if he repeats the manner of the trees' efforts in a varia-tion of his own, he will at least have partly internalized their import. If they sway (as he first puts it) "deeply" and "loudly," he will confer a further stylistic manner on them, twice, in "Eng-lish" words new to the language, to signify that he knows that the trees are speaking nature's foreign words, not his own; but he will force his English meanings to accommodate the trees' wordless vocalise, trying on his new invented words deriving from the trees' own sound: "Deeplier, deeplier, loudlier, loud-lier." The red lines drawn by my computer under these words, telling me that they are not English, make Stevens's point; but now they have been humanized, have become part of a poem in English. By remaining defeated in articulation until the penul-timate line of the poem—as he had in "The Plain Sense of Things"—Stevens maintains a high stylistic tension. What Da-vid can oppose himself to the Goliath of the North Wind? But precisely by interjecting a recognizable, if illiterate, flicker of the human into the depth and volume of the boreal effect, he has at least endorsed the hope that he can turn the repetitive static noise of swaying into something articulate approaching saying.

Stevens's last looks, as I said earlier, were directed not only toward the stasis of the end but also toward its biological hor-ror. If the weight of static depression burdens "The Plain Sense of Things" and "The Region November," it is terror and anger that occasion "Madame La Fleurie," Stevens's poem of the interface of life and death at its most appalling. Stevens is aghast as he is granted a vision showing him that "Mother Nature" is not the flowering and benign inamorata she had seemed to him even in his middle age, when (in "The Man with the Blue Guitar") he praised the moments when we become relatives of her flora and fauna, "when we choose to play / The imagined pine, the imagined jay." Now Madame La Fleurie is "the waiting parent" of his end; he sees that she is a monster who will devour him, along with his mistaken perceptions, his knowledge, and his language. The "great weightings of the end," induced by her "waiting" for her prey, are preparing to press him into an underground grave, where the attendant stars of nature will seal his coffin, and the moon will draw him into her cold sleep. The poet's blue guitar has metamorphosed into a black instrument with thick strings, uttering guttural stutters instead of song.

"Madame La Fleurie" is at first addressed to nature's attendant stars as the poet (spoken of in the third person) sinks toward sleep. But afterward, as he lies in the earth, he sees nature as she has become, a sexually ambiguous and cannibalistic mother:

> Weight him down, O side-stars, with the great
>   weightings of the end.
> Seal him there. He looked in a glass of the earth and
>   thought he lived in it.
> Now, he brings all that he saw into the earth, to the
>   waiting parent.
> His crisp knowledge is devoured by her, beneath a dew.
>
> Weight him, weight, weight him with the sleepiness of
>   the moon.
> It was only a glass because he looked in it. It was
>   nothing he could be told.

It was a language he spoke, because he must, yet did not
know.
It was a page he had found in the handbook of
heartbreak.

The black fugatos are strumming the blacknesses of
black.
The thick strings stutter the finial gutturals.
He does not lie there remembering the blue-jay, say the
jay.
His grief is that his mother should feed on him, himself
and what he saw,
In that distant chamber, a bearded queen, wicked in her
dead light.

How has the last look into death's horror—into what the
poet "saw, / In that distant chamber"—been reproduced stylistically? The first thing one notices on the page is the sheer
weight of the unfamiliarly long lines;[5] and the second is that
the last stanza has five lines, rather than the four of the preceding two, so that the damning vision of the mythical and monstrous mother is held off until the moment after the poem
"should" have finished. I have said that this is Stevens's poem
about the horror of death, a horror of a live burial so unimaginable that he can confront it only obliquely and symbolically,
by remembering legends like that of Bluebeard's Castle. To
sustain ghastliness throughout the silent burial, he stages successive destructions, line by line, of what he has believed about
his life and work. He was wrong about his relation to where he
lived, when he believed that earth was the mirror of thought.
He was wrong about nature as fostering mother, as he sees his
crisp knowledge devoured by her. He was wrong about the objectivity of his insights: "It was only a glass because he looked
in it." He did not truly know the very language he spoke, and

when he begins to speak it in the wake of such deadly admissions, his shattered state deforms his words, twisting fugues into "fugatos," "final" into the visual "finial." His music becomes a tautological speechlessness, enunciating "the blacknesses of black." His final double grief is, yes, that the earth will (in an echo of Shakespeare's "Poor soul") feed on him, but also that he will have had to learn the excruciating "extra" single-line truth: that nature is wicked, unnatural, a "bearded queen" like Macbeth's witches, and that the light in her under-earth chamber is a dead light. Stevens's brusquely phrased sentences take look after look at the worst, as almost every line in the poem shows something being destroyed, while the stanzas prepare for the cumulative vision; and the slowness of the weighty lines ensures that we register, one by one, every single destruction.

Yet there are two voices to this poem. One, as we have seen, speaks the dreadful facts in crisp dismissive sentences: "It was only a glass because he looked in it. It was nothing he could be told." That factual voice sustains the evil of the end. But the other voice sings an incantatory lullaby, "Weight him down, O side-stars, with the great weightings of the end. . . . / Weight him, weight, weight him with the sleepiness of the moon." This is the musical and elegiac voice of the strumming of the black fugatos, of the gutturals of the thick strings. The last three lines, after the final mention of music, impute a consciousness to the poet's corpse; these lines are not themselves song, not even a memory of the song of the blue jay, but commentary. At last the man knows the whole truth, of his own earth-burial and of nature's monstrous appetite for human bodies. Surprisingly, instead of the rage, or fear, or abjectness that he has so far expressed, Stevens meets this truth with grief. "Grief" is an unexpected word to find here; yet when we hear it, we recognize it as the response that can harbor not only the destructive dimensions of the mother but also the lullaby cadences (suggesting her persistent maternity) of the final song.

The horror, that second grim premise of the end-stage in Stevens, appears again when the dove of "'The Dove in Spring" finds itself in a dark dungeon, "deep beneath its walls." The dove, for Stevens, is always an amalgam of the dove of Venus and the dove of the Holy Spirit, symbolizing the poet's two sources of energy, the libido and the imagination. The now-imprisoned dove wonders whether there is another, better world, where there would exist a great outer bush in which it could perch and coo; but even as it speculates, it doubts. The "stripes of silver" created by its prison bars are like strips, like slits of a dungeon window, allowing only a straitened view of a possible alternate "place / And state of being large and light." (One is reminded of Waller's "chinks" that admit light.) The dove is too miserable to coo; it can only howl. It howls against its fate—"that in which it is and that in which it is established"—asking how it can maintain an identity as a dove without a dove's necessities—light and air and a bush to nest in. The pressure of the last days, and the certainty of perpetual imprisonment "deep beneath" the level of natural life, drive Stevens to describe himself as both dove and man, to represent an overlap in which spirit and body are separate but identical:

> Brooder, brooder, deep beneath its walls—
> A small howling of the dove
> Makes something of the little there,
>
> The little and the dark, and that
> In which it is and that in which
> It is established. There the dove

Makes this small howling, like a thought
That howls in the mind or like a man
Who keeps seeking out his identity

In that which is and is established. . . . It howls
Of the great sizes of an outer bush
And the great misery of the doubt of it,

Of stripes of silver that are strips
Like slits across a space, a place
And state of being large and light.

There is this bubbling before the sun,
This howling at one's ear, too far
For daylight and too near for sleep.

Five times the howl of inarticulate pain sounds out, five times
afflicting the poet's ear, keeping him from sleeping yet not ush-
ering in any dawn. If "The Plain Sense of Things" and "Madame La Fleurie" occur in deathly silence, and "The Region
November" in a place of inhuman sound uttered by unintelligible trees, "The Dove in Spring" takes place in the moment of
torture when only a wordless cry of misery can burst from the
spirit, in a howling recurring again and again until consciousness itself is only that animal outcry of the imprisoned libido.
There is no ending of the cry, neither by sleep nor by the arrival
of dawn. No bird is supposed to "howl": it is a violation of its
vocation to musical utterance. Stevens's dove of the spirit has
no chinks and no light in her bodily dungeon; hers are only
imagined chinks, stripes and strips and slits of another space,
an inaccessible region large and light. The howling of the dove
"makes something of the little there," but "something" has the
same unintelligible linguistic indefiniteness as the howl.

We have seen Stevens's last look at the repetitive stasis of age in "The Plain Sense of Things" and "The Region November," and his last look at the horror of live burial in "Madame La Fleurie" and "The Dove in Spring." Even in these last looks at the worst, life demands that the poet, because he is still alive, intuit some cognitive mitigation: the rat comes out to see, life is taught the new tree-language of "deeplier, loudlier," the stars evoke a lullaby of requiem, and the dove yearns for her lonely imaginings of a better place. Besides the two Stevensian premises of the end-stage already described, stasis and horror, there is, as I mentioned earlier, a third premise, a third structure of reality imagined by Stevens's last looks. Against the worst moments—of absence, stasis, wordlessness, and horror—Stevens calls on life and the memory of life for a compensating structure more powerful than the rat, the maternal star-requiem, or the dreamed-of great bush. My example of Stevens's entropic structure and compensating counter-structure is Part I of "The Rock," Stevens's title poem for the last grouping of verses in the *Collected Poems*. Stevens entitled Part I of "The Rock" *Seventy Years Later*. This is Stevens's seventieth-birthday poem, a retrospective examination of his biblically long life. At first, he colorlessly reviews his past—the house of his parents (still extant, but empty, the inhabitants dead), his animal freedom in childhood, his music on the guitar, his early poems, and the embrace of marriage; in retrospect it all seems distant, unreal, impossibly removed. Who knew, in youth, that falling in love was not one's own doing but merely an evolutionary imperative, the sun's way of keeping itself content? The rescue by love seemed so lucky: you made your way from your parents' house to the edge of your field, and your beloved found her way from her parents' house to the edge of her field, and at the border you fell into each other's arms. Or so it seemed at the time; but now? Is there a truer description descried by age?

The past that had seemed so certain and solid is now declared, by the poet at seventy, to be wholly deceptive, an illusion invented to deny actuality. Stevens's theme generates here the first of two sorts of sentences in the poem. The first set is brittle, aphoristic, and brief:

> It is an illusion that we were ever alive,
> Lived in the houses of mothers, arranged ourselves
> By our own motions in a freedom of air.
>
> Regard the freedom of seventy years ago.
> It is no longer air. The houses still stand,
> Though they are rigid in rigid emptiness.
>
> Even our shadows, their shadows, no longer remain.
> The lives these lived in the mind are at an end.
> They never were.... The sounds of the guitar
>
> Were not and are not. Absurd. The words spoken
> Were not and are not. It is not to be believed.

Having denied the reality of his childhood and his music, the poet extends his denials even to romantic love, but as he speaks of love, the sentences, instead of shrinking as they had done earlier, begin to lengthen:

> The meeting at noon at the edge of the field seems like
>
> An invention, an embrace between one desperate clod
> And another in a fantastic consciousness,
> In a queer assertion of humanity:
>
> A theorem proposed between the two—
> Two figures in a nature of the sun,
> In the sun's design of its own happiness....

Stevens's unqualified assertions at the beginning of this poem are the most extreme he has ever made, doing violence to life, his own above all: "It is an illusion that we were ever alive." He has been speaking in a posthumous voice, seeing even his past marriage as a theorem: a geometric hypothesis that two things equal to a third thing, marriage, are equal to each other—or something of that sort. Everything now is denatured, stripped of vitality, emptied out. The style that Stevens evolves to express this absence of life juggles with words such as "illusion," "no longer," "emptiness," and "at an end": these combine with the copulas "were not and are not" to extirpate from existence any nouns—houses, freedom, shadows, lives, sounds, words—as soon as they move into visibility on the page. The sentences are curt; the commentary scornful: "Absurd"; "It is not to be believed."

But this poem—the most nihilistic in Stevens's work so far—begins to wake into a peculiar momentum as soon as the poet entertains the idea of the sun's cosmic sponsorship of marriage. Stevens begins to think of the universe's impersonal nothingness as having a will. It wills to create, against its own eternity, transience; against its own lifelessness, life; against its permanent cold, warmth. It is the mobile universe itself that sponsors the illusion he has been denigrating: the universe, by means of the sun, creates spring, and leaves, and lilacs, and blooming, and the musk of sex, until its own cold permanence is kindled into spring activity, "an incessant being alive." The man and his wife were

Two figures in a nature of the sun,
In the sun's design of its own happiness,

As if nothingness contained a métier,
A vital assumption, an impermanence
In its permanent cold, an illusion so desired

That the green leaves came and covered the high rock,
That the lilacs came and bloomed, like a blindness cleaned,
Exclaiming bright sight, as it was satisfied,

In a birth of sight.

As Stevens recalls his youth—the ecstatic flowering and sexual warmth of spring, the cleansing of his earlier blindness of adolescent isolation, the brightness and satisfaction radiating as he beholds the beloved—his former retrospective dismissals vanish, and he is once again, even at the canonical age of seventy, deep in the moment of embrace, the past moment now not looked at from a frigid distance, as before, but conveyed in the heady immersion of recovered sensation, an ecstatic instance of recollected emotion.

The sentence generating this resurrective memory contends passionately against the desiccation of the earlier syntax of non-existence. Beginning with the meeting at noon, a single long sentence cascades down the page, gaining momentum as it goes, with explanatory phrases, multiple objects, nouns in apposition, successive verbals ("came and covered," "came and bloomed," "exclaiming bright sight"), and continued repetition now not static but dynamic ("Exclaiming bright sight . . . / In a birth of sight"). The transformation will not stop until it is finished, until the formerly despised "desperate clods," male and female, are restored to their youthful senses. Once the feelings of the ardent past have resuscitated themselves, the poet can judge the aliveness of sexual desire differently, not with the "Absurd" of chilly contempt, but with a participatory reprise:

The blooming and the musk
Were being alive, an incessant being alive,
A particular of being, that gross universe.

The universe is no longer "nothingness" but being, a "gross" universe offering flowering, the scent of sex, fertility, beauty, and abundance. There is no better example in lyric poetry of the recapturing of kindled emotion as one relives the sense of being young and being in love; and as Stevens reenters that moment, he revives his consciousness from its former remote and almost posthumous state; the knowledge of death is for a moment eclipsed, not by further illusion (as of an afterlife) but by actual sense memory. The gratitude with which Stevens realizes that he can still feel his past, not merely survey it, closes his seventieth-birthday retrospect. Style has respected—by its mutation around the hinge of repudiated but then resuscitated marriage—both the aridity of age and the elasticity of regained vitality. This last look can hold at its interface both contempt and joy.

There are many more last looks in the collection called *The Rock*, and they crowd my memory asking for a recognition that space will not allow. When Stevens said, "Farewell, my days," in the poem "Farewell without a Guitar," he was repeating, with the word "farewell," a diction echoing his English predecessors. But in the poems I have singled out here, he finds, in the tragic end-stage of life, modern and disturbing styles of farewell, both structural and stylistic, which delineate not only the stasis, horror, and unreality of that end-stage but also its inquisitive appetite for knowledge, its lullabies in the midst of burial, and, even in its worst mental *rigor mortis*, the unexpected and solacing sensual warmth of memory.

3

The Contest of Melodrama and Restraint:
Sylvia Plath's *Ariel*

In Sylvia Plath's juvenilia, we can see that the chief danger to her style is restraint: formality encases her emotions. And yet her style was endangered equally—once she allowed emotion its freedom—by a theatricalizing melodrama. Both of these dangers always hovered over her poetry, and no one—as we can see in her journals and letters—was more aware of their perils than she. She died a suicide at thirty, but the fact of death, and death as a subject of expression, had preoccupied her from the time she was eight, when her father died in a fashion inexplicable to a child. Although Otto Plath was a professor of entomology, he convinced himself that the illness he was experiencing was cancer and refused medical attention. In fact, he had suffered adult-onset diabetes and could have been successfully treated. By the time he was hospitalized, one leg had become gangrenous, and he died of sepsis. (It seems probable, in retrospect, that it was the clinical depression that eventually doomed his daughter that caused Otto Plath to lie in bed for months before he died.) According to Plath's account in "Lady Lazarus," her father's death caused her to attempt suicide at the age of ten; when she tried it again at nineteen, she almost succeeded. After her college suicide attempt, Plath was treated with painful electroshock and varied medications; she also underwent the psychotherapy of the time, which, because it encouraged a dwelling on childhood trauma, may have helped to fix Otto Plath's death in his daughter's mind as the ineradicable cause of her own rage, melancholy, and instability. Her death wish permeates even her Smith College juvenilia; she practiced taking the last look from the time she began to write.

Although Plath's early fantasies of death are concealed under impersonal carapaces, they seem in hindsight transparently autobiographical. In a youthful Audenesque sonnet, "The Trial of Man," Plath, addressing "man" in general as "you," asserts, "You were condemned to serve the legal limit / And burn to death within your neon hell." The poem ends with "man" grotesquely awaiting electrocution:

> Now, disciplined in the strict ancestral chair,
>   You sit, solemn-eyed, about to vomit,
> The future an electrode in your skull.[1]

Other early fantasies are even more violent. The somewhat incoherent "Sonnet: To Eva" begins,

> All right, let's say you could take a skull and break it
> The way you'd crack a clock; you'd crush the bone
> Between steel palms of inclination, take it,
> Observing the wreck of metal and rare stone.

The effects of death on Plath's style were, as such an example reveals, at times disastrous. Melodrama and the depiction of violence—restrained in the poem above only by Plath's sonnet rigidities—were two of the stylistic results of her traumatized view of existence, but they coexisted with a jeering irony, visible in Plath's damning inventory of herself as Eva in the same sonnet. She is an unmendable mechanical Humpty Dumpty, composed of a heap of intractable and platitudinous metallic organs—

> Cogs and disks, inane mechanic whims,
> And idle coils of jargon yet unspoken.

Not man nor demigod could put together
The scraps of rusted reverie, the wheels
Of notched tin platitudes concerning weather,
Perfume, politics, and fixed ideals.[2]

How was Plath—without ruining her poems—to retain
authentic features of her imagination, such as the symbols of
melodrama and violence absorbed from her childhood literary
matrix of legends, fairy tales, and catastrophic myths from
Bluebeard to Dracula? Plath's later interesting revisions of
these theatrical *dramatis personae* created them as ambiguous
characters, so that the melodrama is generated by a conflict in
which no clear moral discrimination can be made between pro-
tagonist and antagonist. Plath herself could only rarely play the
part of an innocent victim; she felt more honest, in her most
conspicuously staged poems, when playing the man-eating
Lady Lazarus pitting her obscene striptease against her voy-
euristic audience, or the vampire-killing daughter vanquishing
the vampire parent in "Daddy."

For a long time, "death" meant to Sylvia Plath only the
twinned images of her father's malignant gangrenous toe and
her own envisaged suicide. Death lived within her, estranging
her not only from herself but also from other human beings,
including her widowed mother, for whom she felt obliged to
play the role of a happy and successful daughter. Plath's violent
death dramas do not dominate every poem she wrote, but because they recurred as insistent imaginative material, she
needed to find vehicles for them that could be vehicles of art.
She is candid about the exaggeration of the images that throng
her mind and works hard toward the end of her life to find
forms of restraint that will not betray the excruciating content
of her poems and to find images of tragic being that will not

wreck aesthetic shape. As we see her last looks at death, we can trace her arrival, through a deepening mastery of technique, at a poetic strength absent in her earliest work. Although I begin with a few glances at early poems, I will spend most of my time on a single sequence by Plath, "Berck-Plage," which seems to me to illustrate both her inability to remove death from her poetry and her eventual success at integrating it stylistically with her aesthetic aims.

As an artist, Plath explicitly desired four things: honesty of perception, clarity of analysis, discipline of expression, and moral strength. These desires, raised to principles, pervade even her juvenilia. In "Notes to a Neophyte," she issues over-alliterating commands to an apprentice self judged to be too unrestrained, too vague, too falsely social:

> metamorphose the mollusk
> of vague vocabulary
> with structural discipline;
> stiffen the ordinary
> malleable mask
> to the granite grin of bone.

Unhappily, such a passage sums up clarity, discipline, and strength in a linguistically embarrassing surfeit of metamorphosing mollusks and granite grins. As for acquiring honesty, that was more difficult. At first, Plath took the task of honesty to be a satiric one: to expose, with sadistic satisfaction, the clay feet of the patriarchal idols of the tribe:

> our eyes glut
> themselves on the clay toes and short clubfoot
> which mar the idol's sanctity.

To confine honesty to the unmasking of social fraud, however, is to follow too easy a path, since it excludes honesty directed at the self. Plath proceeds in this early poem, "Metamorphoses of the Moon," to a question far more important for her future work: how to choose the more honest of two equally plausible views. Here she debates the choice between imaginative and scientific representations of the moon:

> The choice between the mica mystery
> of moonlight or the pockmarked face we see
>   through the scrupulous telescope
> is always to be made: innocence
> is a fairy-tale; intelligence
>   hangs itself on its own rope.

In subsequent works, Plath balances between a diction of innocence—which, under the terrors of suffering, regresses to a childlike belief in angels and ogres—and a diction of intelligence, which is scrupulous with respect to external fact. Honesty to trauma, early and late, required of her both the admission of the child's melodramatic volatility and the representation of the adult's discriminating scrutiny.

Some critics have thought that Plath failed to maintain an equal respect for feeling and fact. When—in an attempt to show the annihilating pain visited upon her at eight by her father's self-willed suicide—she compared him to a Nazi and herself to a Jew, she was criticized for appropriating for her own circumstances a fact too historically large, and too exclusively the property of the murdered Jews, to be contracted out to private domestic loss. Such a metaphor seemed to some a failure of adult judgment, however accurate it might be to Plath's inner conviction that in willing his own death, her father had killed her too; as she said at his grave in "Electra on Azalea Path," "The day you died I went into the dirt." Plath failed in a similar way, some believed, when, instead of inserting herself into the image of the exalted Lazarus, raised from the dead, she converted him to her own purposes, changing him into herself, a malevolent "Lady Lazarus." I mention these criticisms of Plath's melodramas of appropriation because they have been leveled by serious lovers of poetry. Others—myself among them—do not find a failure of morality or tact in Plath's extreme metaphors. Her German father, she thought, had murdered her own will to live by caring too little for her to attempt to save his own life. It is undeniable that her sickening death drive (which she ascribed, perhaps mistakenly, to her father's willed dying) never left her mind; she had recurrent violent nightmares of "destruction, annihilations— / An assembly-line of cut throats" ("Waking in Winter"). In such circumstances, with such feelings, no moderate metaphor could be accurate. When she was resurrected, at nineteen, from a near-death state (after an overdose of barbiturates), it was natural that the myth of Lazarus should come to her mind. Unlike Lazarus, however, Plath returned not to joy but to horror: confinement in a hospital, electroshock, shame, public disgrace; and she endured those events while wanting still, and always, to die. How could she have imagined herself into the fate of the real Lazarus, happily restored to his family?

The harsh critiques of Plath's poems of violence and melodrama bear witness not only to the disturbing force with which the death drive grasped her being but also to her success in transmitting that force in aggressive language. It needs to be remembered that she was a more exigent critic of herself than any commentator has been. Her last poems reveal that she had resolved to adopt a volume other than the *fortissimo* of "Daddy" and "Lady Lazarus." Still young in her art, she aimed, as we shall see, at aesthetic control and moderation of expression in spite of the death-obsession within which she had to live and create.

The worst thing her early trauma did to the adult Plath was

to deprive her of both past and future. She had no real past, in her view, because she had always (since coming to self-consciousness at the age of eight) been dead; and she had no real future because she foresaw only an unrelieved continuation of the "neon hell" of nightmare in which she perpetually lived. Although past and future tenses appear in Plath's juvenilia, they become rare in her adult poems, which take place in an acute and electric present. The strongest demand placed on Plath's style by its confinement to the present moment was that it keep that moment charged and progressive even in its temporal immobility. Since the creation in a poem of panels of time—past, present, and future—is one of the strongest ways to simulate a believable human speaker, Plath is forced, by her fixed incarceration in the present, toward other means of self-construction. The creation of an insistent and isolated "I," surrounded by brilliant images, is her most frequent choice of means. The classic case of that present-tense "I," mythologized as Godiva, can be seen in Plath's suicidal coursing into the sun as her horse Ariel rises from earth to air. As she rides, she becomes stripped of all but the pure active will of the vital "I," which dictates to the poem called "Ariel" its unrelenting high tessitura:

> White
> Godiva, I unpeel——
> Dead hands, dead stringencies.
>
> And now I
> Foam to wheat, a glitter of seas.
> The child's cry
>
> Melts in the wall.
> And I
> Am the arrow,

The dew that flies
Suicidal, at one with the drive
Into the red

Eye, the cauldron of morning.

We experience a sense of gasping relief when the prolonged and repeated high pitch of the "I" sound, sustained by its ten instances (from "White" to "I"), subsides into the lower vowels of the incinerating sun, "the cauldron of morning." In this wonderfully managed poem of the present-tense "I," the "I" strips itself, image by image, until it aims itself out of itself.

In "Ariel," as in other late theatrical poems of the "I," Plath achieves an increasing reining in of her tendency to the ostentatiously lurid. She could not do without it—the lurid cannot be easily deleted from her conception of dying—but she could manage it without restricting it within the cage of a grotesque sonnet, without the gothic stage machinery of "Daddy" and "Lady Lazarus." Plath did more than put reins on her "I"; she began to be morally capable of what she named, in the title of a poem, as "The Courage of Shutting Up." Although there are "disks of outrage" in the mind of the surgeon-protagonist of that poem, he does not speak, and his eyes refrain from sending out their death rays:

The surgeon is quiet, he does not speak.
He has seen too much death, his hands are full of it. . . .

. . . the tongue, too, has been put by.

But how about the eyes, the eyes, the eyes?

Their death rays [are] folded like flags
Of a country no longer heard of,
An obstinate independency
Insolvent among the mountains.

In "shutting up," refusing to wield the death rays of her dominant "I's," Plath acquired a new style. It appears in various short poems that have become famous, such as "Edge." But the poem in which her impersonal style is extensively and brilliantly displayed is a June 1962 sequence called "Berck-Plage," which preceded by a few months the vow of silence in "The Courage of Shutting Up." Of the 126 lines of "Berck-Plage," only seven contain "I" or "my";[3] reading the poem, one senses a sharp change from Plath's "I" mode. "Berck-Plage" is a poem in which, though using "ultimate" words and images, Plath maintains, through descriptive objectivity, a moral equilibrium. In "Berck-Plage" Plath allows herself theatricality and violence while putting them under the sponsorship of intelligence, creating a detachment in which a last look is sanely, if despairingly, directed toward natural death. Plath could write "Berck-Plage" so well because she had turned her attention away from herself and her father, and had written about natural death, not suicide. The poem commemorates the death of her aged neighbor, Percy Key, who had been pictured in the April poem "Among the Narcissi" as an "octogenarian . . . recuperating from something on the lung." Commenting on the stoic courage of Key's walking on the hill where he "nurses the hardship of his stitches," Plath perceives that "there is a dignity to this; there is a formality." It was that dignity and formality that she carried into the composition of "Berck-Plage."

"Berck-Plage" fuses, as Ted Hughes notes, the 1962 death and funeral of Percy Key with a 1961 visit that he and Sylvia Plath made to a beach in Normandy called Berck-Plage—the location of a hospital serving cancer patients, amputees, and victims of accidents, who took their exercise on the beach.[4] Several of Plath's obsessions are incorporated into "Berck-Plage": her father (with his emblematic black shoe for the gangrenous foot) displaced into the person of the village priest (also, of course, called "Father," making the implicit link); Otto Plath's grave (earlier described in "Electra on Azalea Path"); the sea as an abyss swallowing living things, out of which once-living things, now dead, are hauled; hills as stable presences in contrast to the devouring sea; ritual; sexual infidelity; corpses and their remains; eternity; and disappearance. But "Berck-Plage" is helped toward a stance of contemplation by its leisurely construction as a sequence (it has seven equal parts, each made up of nine couplets). The terrible attraction to death is here, but Plath's stylistic response on this occasion is to represent death in slow motion; although the poem takes last looks at several stages of death, ending in a pilgrimage to a grave, there are many nearly static scenes on its path to that "naked mouth."

Before coming to the individual parts of "Berck-Plage," I must give a brief sketch of its two-part plot, in which the presence of the lyric speaker as a person is minimal. In the first part, which takes place at the seashore, the speaker, partly healthy, unlike the hospital amputees ("I have two legs"), but partly ill of an "inflammation," walks by the sea, observing the black-cassocked figure of Death the priest as well as the mackerel gatherers' dead fish, geometrized into "black and green lozenges." While the merciless priest (after the manner of Otto Plath the professor) obliviously reads a book, two lovers embrace behind former wartime concrete bunkers. The sea, feared by the speaker, is full of corpses that it has swallowed, and its entangling weeds seem like hairy private parts. Frightened not only by the menacing sea but also by the hotel-hospital for the sick and the maimed, the speaker recuses herself from responsibility to the diseased and dying.

The second part of "Berck-Plage," taking place inland, occupies itself with Plath's dead neighbor. Individual sections represent Percy Key's embalming at the undertaker's, then his body in the coffin, together with the coffin bearers and the engraved date on the coffin plaque. Subsequently, the widow and her daughters keep vigil in their stone house at evening; in the morning, the funeral takes place in the presence of priest, widow, daughters, and speaker. Although the soul, in a glance at Christian iconography, is transmuted to a bride, the husband is not Christ, as conventional belief would have it, but the gaping earth. Finally, the burial in the cemetery is described through the eyes of children on a neighboring hill. They see, in their distorted vision from above, hats superimposed flatly on the grass as if their wearers had magically disappeared. This remote view staves off for a moment the act of burial; but as the poem arrives at the naked mouth of the grave, the plasma of hope in the mourning speaker runs out, and death is confirmed in gaping despair.

Plath's stylistic response to Percy Key's death, as I have said, is to invent an impersonal style. What does a piece of that style "feel like"? Not only has it put aside those piercing "I's" in favor of objective description, it has also put aside (for the most part) the excitable questions and exclamations that normally attend Plath's anxiety-ridden "I." With the courage of shutting up, the tongue of the poem has been quieted. The facts in the undertaker's parlor are few: the dead man has been embalmed and placed in a coffin; the sick-bed nurses have lost their function; the corpse's hands are folded; the sheets and pillow cases of the deathbed have been washed; a silver plaque with the date engraved on it has been affixed to the oak coffin. As I have summarized them, the facts are emotionless. Plath's charge to herself, in writing the poem, is to surround death with interpretation and emotion, but to do so without permitting the continual intrusion of the personal "I." The speaker is allowed to make remarks, but they are chiefly the remarks not of an "I" but of an "eye," an eye that can speak of what it sees but must restrict itself to copulative verbs of constatation, without verbs of personal action. Here are the flat opening phrases of section 4 of "Berck-Plage," representing the embalmed Percy Key:

A wedding-cake face in a paper frill.
How superior he is now.

It is like possessing a saint.
The nurses in their wing-caps are no longer so beautiful.

They are browning, like touched gardenias.
The bed is rolled from the wall.

This is what it is to be complete. It is horrible.

After the summary outburst "It is horrible," the pure flatness of observation cannot persist; but even as the imagination raises its queries, and the personality of the speaker intrudes itself, a macabre decorum is maintained at the wake:

Is he wearing pajamas or an evening suit

Under the glued sheet from which his powdery beak
Rises so whitely unbuffeted?

They propped his jaw with a book until it stiffened
And folded his hands, that were shaking, goodbye,
  goodbye.

Now the washed sheets fly in the sun,
The pillow cases are sweetening.

It is a blessing, it is a blessing:
The long coffin of soap-colored oak,

The curious bearers and the raw date
Engraving itself in silver with marvelous calm.

Imitating the "marvelous calm" of the self-engraving date (except for the spurt of revulsion in "It is horrible"), the speaker stands in the undertaker's parlor taking the mourner's last look at the corpse. Sight is the only sense drawn upon (with the single exception of "The pillow cases are sweetening"). The speaker restricts herself to only two binding forces in her eighteen lines: the copulative verb "is" ("are," "were"), which appears twelve times, and the terminal "-ing," employed ten times. The inert copula is the sign of the impotence of the eye to change anything; the "-ing" endings agitate the lines into a progressive present in order to give the corpse-picture the illusion of motion. The only departure from the intense present moment comes in the two past-tense lines about the preparation of the body, when real actions could still occur: "They propped his jaw . . . / And folded his hands."

Restricted to being an eye, the speaker is immobile in body; having decided on reticence, she is contained, almost tongueless. Her images must speak for her emotions, except for the few moments in which her tongue cannot be restrained from exclamation or comment: "How superior he is now"; "It is horrible"; "The pillow cases are sweetening"; "It is a blessing, it is a blessing." The sole question of this section—"What lies under that glued sheet?"—cannot be satisfied, but the wish to know causes the poem's flashback to aspects formerly knowable: the open jaw (before the "beautification" of embalming) and the shaking hands (when the corpse was alive). The stanza's three-line initial query ("Is he wearing pajamas or an evening suit," etc.) matches the second three-line segment at the close ("The long coffin," etc.). These three-line segments stand out from the others, which occupy one or two lines. The opening one-line, one-fact noun phrase of the affixed eye ("A wedding-cake face") matches in its nominal, verbless form the three-line, three-fact noun phrase, with the eye similarly affixed, of the close: "The long coffin ... , // The curious bearers ... the raw date / Engraving itself." The calm of the self-engraving date is "marvelous" only because it repudiates a personal dirge, as the poet strives to do. The face in the frill is seen with the cold eye that in youth noticed the "pockmarked face" of the moon; evasive "mica mystery" has no place here. Plath does permit herself brief relentings into lyric farewell, "goodbye, goodbye," and into the lulling ritual words "It is a blessing, it is a blessing." Underneath that soothing music, however, lies a suppressed outcry: the "raw" date that signifies extinction proclaims itself flayed into being.

"What is the name of that color?" the speaker of "Berck-Plage" asks as she sees the earth into which Percy Key will be lowered. She answers herself in another succession of noun phrases, this time images of post-traumatic aftermath: "Old blood of caked walls the sun heals, / Old blood of limb stumps, burnt hearts." If the immediate artery spurt of the blood jet is poetry ("Kindness"), then these images of old blood on healed walls, old blood of earlier amputations (such as Plath's father's), and calcined hearts from a fire now cold, tell us that Plath sees the possibility of a style that is not a present-tense outburst resembling a jet from a living wound but a style that is more diagnostic, more measured, speaking after the fact about the caked walls, the stitched stump, the charred heart. She maintains this style with admirable evenness throughout "Berck-Plage," regaining it after every protest that escapes her lips. It is only at the end, as the cortège arrives at Percy Key's grave, that the style breaks down utterly and the blood jet returns, this time as a sky pouring out the last of its life-giving plasma. All claims of "marvelous calm" unravel, as we see, through the children's wondering eyes, first the geometrized bearers and coffin, but then the naked wound of the open grave:

Six round black hats in the grass and a lozenge of
    wood
And a naked mouth, red and awkward.

For a minute the sky pours into the hole like plasma.
There is no hope, it is given up.

The final ironic and earnest echo of "consummatum est," breaking from the speaker's mouth, confirms the irreversibility of the end.

Plath has, then, found in her late style two manners of taking the "last look": the blood-jet cry of the "I" and the post-traumatic analysis by the eye. The first manner has more continuity with the poet's earlier work; the second represents, in Tim Kendall's words, "a new style."[5] Death envisaged as already accomplished creates the severer manner, in which, no longer imprisoned in an agonizing present tense, Plath assumes a retrospective stance. Her own comment on the new style presents itself in the poem "Words," dated February 1, ten days before Plath's death on February 11. In "Words," the old wounds suffered in the past return in transfigured form in the present; the ax strokes of traumatic tree fellings in the past send off present echoes, which sound like hoofbeats:

Axes
After whose stroke the wood rings,
And the echoes!
Echoes traveling
Off from the center like horses.

Suddenly Plath abandons these present-tense short-phrased echoes for a long visual narrative of past tears and their aftermath, retold in a different present tense, that of the newly felled tree:

> The sap
> Wells like tears, like the
> Water striving
> To re-establish its mirror
> Over the rock
>
> That drops and turns,
> A white skull,
> Eaten by weedy greens.

The "granite grin" of the juvenile "Notes to a Neophyte" reappears here in the rock as skull, the foundation over which tears run, as the psyche strives to reestablish in the form of water its original sap/jet, which will, as it abates its motion, become a still mirror of contemplative reflection.

With no transition, Plath returns from her feelings at the time of her felling to the echoes created by her subsequent representation of that trauma in words:

> Years later I
> Encounter them on the road—
>
> Words dry and riderless,
> The indefatigable hoof-taps.

With the word "indefatigable," Plath claims permanence for her poem. The poem "should" end here, with this understated but identifiable boast: normally, "eternizing" assurances end the poems in which they appear. But Plath, with another unannounced transition to tears, reveals that the sap/tears/water has indeed reestablished its pool, but not a reflective one:

> While
> From the bottom of the pool, fixed stars
> Govern a life.

The striking images of this poem—axes to sap to tears to falling water to rock to skull to pool to fixed stars—have attracted
the fine attention of Tim Kendall, Plath's best critic. But I want
to consider here a different aspect of this late poem, in which,
though the tree/poet dies into a skull, the indefatigable hoof-
taps continue into a solid future. The aspect to which I turn is
Plath's construction of sentences.

In Plath's narrative of the tree/poet, both prelude (lines
1–5) and coda (lines 14–20) consist of two sentences, but the
tale of the tears (lines 6–13) is voiced in a long single sentence
coursing down the page, imitating the purposive journey of the
tears, as the water acknowledges in turn both the eventual skull
of its former body and even its posthumous destruction by
tempus edax, the devouring "weedy greens." In short, the opening sentences track the initial ringing echoes of words; the long
middle sentence tracks the posthumous life of the sap of the
felled tree; and the last two sentences track the response of a
present self contemplating its own past and future. The "I" appears late in the poem's "dry" close, in the penultimate stanza:
"Years later, I / Encounter [the words] on the road." The weeping of the sap has ceased, the water has disappeared, and even
the rock skull has been devoured by nature. As the poet rereads
her past work, it no longer seems a shriek of active trauma nor
a slow bodily production of tears, but takes on its metrical
character as "indefatigable hoof-taps." Instead of former selves
being shed like "old whore petticoats" (as in "Fever 103°"), or
enduring as skulls or bones, or being consumed by the sun,
they endure as words. It is the last three lines of "Words" that
give pause. Water, we thought, had disappeared with the white
skull and its correlative rock. But no—water reappears, no longer as striving and cursive but as a static pool, itself as immobile as the fixed stars which, normally reflected on the surface

of the water, are interpreted as sunk, unchanging and un-changeable, at the bottom of the pool.[6] The temporal motion of the poem—so important to Plath, as we saw in "Ariel"—is here suspended in the "while" introducing the final "sentence" (an adverbial sentence fragment). "While," always of great use to poets, makes two things happen simultaneously. Plath would have known the power of "while," especially from Keats's ode "To Autumn": "While barrèd clouds bloom the soft-dying day . . . / Then in a wailful choir the small gnats mourn. . . ." As Keats's "while" enables the simultaneity of the visual and the auditory, so Plath's enables the simultaneity of immortal sounds and mortal fate. While the fixed stars of determinism govern an individual life, the indefatigable hoofbeats of human creation simultaneously assert themselves beyond that lifetime. Even the legitimate pride Plath feels with respect to her past work, as she encounters it "years later," cannot extinguish her conviction that her life is not her own to direct.

The present tense of "Words" is, as I have said, ingeniously distributed among Plath's own retrospective present, her present present (in the attempt to reestablish a reflective pool), and the eternal present of the fixed stars. In the sardonic poem "Gigolo," also from this period, the gigolo leans over a pool:

> All the fall of water an eye
> Over whose pool I tenderly
> Lean and see me.

When in "Words" Plath represents the eye regarding the pool, it no longer views its narcissistic image, as in "Gigolo," but rather perceives the ordaining conditions of fate. The objectiv-ity of regard in "Words," as in "Berck-Plage," arises from Plath's adoption of a view that is post-traumatic, even posthumous, but it is a point of view tenaciously maintained as long as the poet is alive. It cools the eye and slows the pace from Ariel's rapidity to water's slow descent; it allows dryness as well as tears; it demands above all a dispassionate diagnosis of how things stand.

On the other hand, a feverish heat within is native to Plath. Can this late dry and cool style be applied to a description of heat? Plath attempted this feat more than once, using flowers—tulips, poppies—as symbols of life heat. "Tulips" is a long exercise in the dry style, but its Lawrentian length links it to a Romantic desire for extended expressiveness that is "moist" rather than "dry." Plath found a more successful binocular vision of death and life in the faultless poem "Poppies in October." In it, the redness of life and the pallor of death engage from the beginning in an antiphonal shadow play, the motion of their interchange speeding up as the poem advances. The poppies—an unexpected "love-gift" to the desolate poet—set the standard for redness with their female "skirts"; their redness surpasses even that of the red dawn-clouds and the red jet of blood staining the coat of a dying woman:

POPPIES IN OCTOBER

Even the sun-clouds this morning cannot manage such
    skirts.
Nor the woman in the ambulance
Whose red heart blooms through her coat so
    astoundingly—

A gift, a love gift
Utterly unasked for
By a sky

Palely and flamily
Igniting its carbon monoxides, by eyes
Dulled to a halt under bowlers.

O my God, what am I
That these late mouths should cry open
In a forest of frost, in a dawn of cornflowers.

27 October 1962

In the implied scenario preceding the poem, Plath, under a wintry dawn sky filled with reddening "sun-clouds," finds herself on a street where poppies are for sale and where businessmen wearing bowler hats are walking by while an ambulance hurtles past, carrying a hemorrhaging woman. The aesthetic poppies, the rosy clouds, the commonplace businessmen, and the bleeding female body compete for Plath's attention. It is to the ravishing beauty of the flowers that the poet responds first; she can describe the poppies adequately, she implies, only by declaring that their "skirts" surpass the sun-clouds, and—as she apparently heartlessly gathers the ambulance patient into her admiration of the shape and color of the flowers—that the poppies' red surpasses the "bloom" of a bursting heart. The patient is solely a spectacle as her coat becomes soaked with an expanding red stain. But suddenly the ambulance seems forgotten as the senses carry Plath into gratitude for the unexpected beauty of the flowers so late in the year; they are a "gift, a love gift." The chill of death—present in the ambulance but warded off by Plath's willfully contemplating only the color of the woman's blood, not its cause—is displaced as Plath transforms the red heat of poppies and lifeblood into the bleak exhaust-oxymoron of the sky, "flamily" (if also "palely") "igniting its carbon monoxides." Lethal in the aftermath of both its igniting sun flame and its igniting wintry clouds, the sky asks for no such gift of beauty, nor do the "halted" souls of the dull-eyed, quasi-dead bowler-wearing men.

Isolated from both sinister landscape and suffering patient by her defensive aesthetic attention, the poet wonders why she

has been chosen as the recipient of this unasked-for but conso-
latory gift; and the poppies, enabling Plath's poetic utterance
by metamorphosing themselves into "late mouths" that "cry
open," create around themselves a paradoxical environment,
composed of a forest of frost that breathes death, and a dawn
of cornflowers that breathes renewal. In the earlier "Poppies in
July," dated July 20, 1962, the poet, assaulted by the red of the
poppies, longed for a deathly colorlessness. The view there is
purely self-enclosed: there are no ambulances, no businessmen,
no clouds. Only when Plath turned to an external reality fram-
ing her emotions was she able to include death objectively, to
see it as something other than a personal assault.

The rhythms of "Poppies in October" derive from the poem's malignant dactylic rendering of the fatal sky "Palely and
flamily / Igniting its carbon monoxides, by eyes / Dulled to a
halt under bowlers." The dactyls even initiate the poem: "Even
the sun-clouds this morning cannot manage such skirts." These
falling rhythms govern all of Plath's local sense perceptions
(skirts, heart, sky), but at the end of the poem they are con-
quered by their opposite, the rising rhythm of anapests, in "O
my God, what am I" and "In a forest of frost, in a dawn of cornflowers." By thus "turning itself inside out" rhythmically, the
poem ends on a note of gratitude. It has first alternated an
alienated aesthetic perception with astonishment at "a love gift,"
but that life benefit has been temporarily obscured by the hostile crematorium sky and the inert robotic eyes under bowlers.
Plath finds herself able to end with renewed exaltation at the
gift of beauty because she has discovered a different rhythm
and a new set of words (unaltered "forest" and "flowers" in lieu
of flowers transmuted into "skirts") that can restore beauty to
nature, not place it cold-heartedly in the context of human
hemorrhage.

If we ask ourselves how Plath found a style with which to

gather death and life into a single binocular view, we can reply that for her the task became specialized, since death was always before her eyes. She needed to discover a way to restore life to the skull, to put blood into the face of death, as George Herbert said. Her melodrama and violence were ways of waking Death up: to make a corpse stand up and do a striptease, to construct an ambulatory black boot over a dead foot. The sheer force of her animating will, as she breathes life into inert clay or tries to reassemble the *disjecta membra* of a father-Colossus, puts the poetry under a strain of energetic artificiality. The interface of life and death becomes a site of manipulated shock electrically galvanizing personified Death into personified Life. Plath's poetry survives aesthetically because Death is so violently present that Life must take on a matching violence, but when their confrontation takes place in a present-tense personal moment, the result, in her mature work, is more a duel than a binocular comprehensiveness. When Plath left aside her own and her father's suicidal drives and contemplated the natural death of Percy Key, she could, while maintaining aspects of the macabre, let her poem "engrave itself" calmly, with Percy Key's formality and dignity as her guide. She learned to examine death with an impersonality of style that announces her eventual critique of poems exclusively personal in utterance. She could maintain her late severity and impersonality by regarding herself from the outside in poems such as "Axes" and "Edge" that succeed in containing life and death within a single steadfast gaze. She could reprove her subordination of human response to aesthetic response in "Poppies in October," chillingly conveying in a dry style the alienated eye describing the hemorrhage, while exhibiting the resuscitation of human feeling in her confession of unworthiness before the gift of beauty. Repentance for her "sin" of aesthetic appropriation of blood lies behind the outburst of penitential gratitude: "O my God, what am I / That these late mouths should cry open." The complex relation between the detached "appreciation" of the red heart-blood and the subsequent penitence before the living poppies makes Plath's confrontation of life and death—in her last look before she will be suffocated by the lethal sky—one that accommodates both her native violence of imagery and her newly objective style. She was always a posthumous person, but it took her years to acquire a posthumous style.

4

_____

Images of Subtraction: Robert Lowell's *Day by Day*

In his last book, *Day by Day*, Robert Lowell, when confronting life with anticipated death, made such poems persuasive by set-ting, against the completions achieved in life, multiple images of subtraction. *Day by Day* was published in September 1977, just before Lowell died, at sixty, of a heart attack. Although his death appeared premature, he had expected its arrival, as his medical history, his poems, and his late letters reveal; both of his parents had died at sixty, and he had already, in January 1977, been hospitalized for congestive heart disease. He had lived impetuously in his last seven years, beginning a love affair in England with Caroline Guinness while still married to his second wife, Elizabeth Hardwick. Caroline Guinness bore a son, Sheridan; Lowell remained in England, he and Hardwick were divorced, and he and Caroline married. Although Low-ell's bipolar illness had been helped in the sixties by lithium (after decades of recurrent breakdowns), in England there was another discouraging episode of mania and confinement in an asylum. In a hospital poem of *Day by Day* ironically entitled "Home," Lowell expects imminent death; noticing the date (January 10, 1976) on the morning paper, he paces the ward,

saying,
as one would instinctively say Hail Mary,
I wish I could die.

> Less than ever I expect to be alive
> six months from now—
> *1976,*
> a date I dare not affix to my grave.[1]

The date affixed to his grave was to be 1977, but here his self-extirpation is immediate and absolute, as he imagines his own dated, incised tombstone, where text substitutes for presence. In the titles of *Day by Day* there are numerous premonitions and prophecies of Lowell's own death and the death of others: "Our Afterlife," "Suicide," "Departure," "Burial," "Endings," and—to close the volume—"Epilogue." The volume contains elegies not only for Lowell's father and mother but also a preemptive elegy for Jean Stafford (Lowell's first wife) and actual elegies for several friends and acquaintances—John Berryman, Israel Citkovitz (Guinness's second husband), and W. H. Auden.[2] *Day by Day* is a volume that takes a last look wherever it casts its eye.

Lowell does attempt, in this final collection, themes countering the premonition of death. Chief among the life themes is the *carpe diem* of his years in England with Caroline Guinness (although their marriage was disintegrating during the years of composition of *Day by Day*, and the poem "Last Walk?" announces its end). Lowell may will to conjecture a future, but his deeply embedded faith in sequential narrative—which made him arrange the sonnets of his volume *History* in chronological order from Adam and Eve to the present—is shaken by the thought that with the approach of death, his life has ceased to create a narrative. His earlier poems were a cavalry charge; now he must tread water.

Can a poet of history in motion invent a style incorporating inertia and death? Lowell's resources in this predicament are many, but a central and successful one—and my topic here—is his unfailing gift for images of his present paradoxical state, of being wildly alive and yet certain of death. He has two methods for finding the telling image: the first is to relinquish continuous narrative in favor of glimpses, and the second is to call attention again and again to subtraction, the unhappy opposite of that basic resource of narrative, addition. In the premise of the title *Day by Day*, Lowell's *ad hoc* images are removed from the flow of a chronological life history (in which they would normally appear one after the other), in favor of anachronistic Poundian montage, in which images of past *and* present, universal *and* particular, succeed each other as if on a flat screen, flashing on the eye in disorienting simultaneity. (By contrast, images of the past in Lowell's most famous book, *Life Studies*, tend to remain enclosed within the past that they described.)

"We were kind of religious," Lowell wrote in closing one of his sonnets, "we thought in images." If we wish to know what Lowell thought, we can find out from the import of his images. Normally, images would be linked by transitions, but *Day by Day* leaps from one image to another without explanation. Because at sixty the poet has his whole past spread out before him and can move easily around and within the panorama, he would falsify that late ease of wide-angle spectatorship if he were to offer justification for his erratic linkages. As we read a poem in *Day by Day*, we must mimic this wandering mind, taking on faith the hope that one piece of the poem has something to do with the others, and that behind all the scattering on offer we can perceive the poet pacing his terrain, taking his last look.

A poet who thinks in images must find a way to render his visual hoard verbal, translating it into the lines and rhythms and formal groupings of verse. The insufficiency of words as representations of images becomes distressing to Lowell as,

with age, the images dwindle, and their linguistic force and solidity fade. Attempting to call to mind images of Jean Stafford,
he grieves:

> How quickly I run through my little set
> of favored pictures ... pictures starved to words.
> My memory economizes so prodigally
> I know I have suffered theft.

As he reviews life's images, the poet of *Day by Day* is perturbed
by how they pale and falter and even disappear in the mental
narrowing that precedes death. This last of Lowell's volumes
derives much of its imaginative energy from the poet's investigation of the items that are being, or have been, subtracted,
thieved, from his life. His investigation must not only enumerate the actual losses but also discover stylistic means to vivify
those now-invisible things that have been subtracted.

Now that history can no longer serve Lowell as a reliable
template for the architectonics of life and poetry, now that
memory, the indispensable aid to history, has suffered theft, the
poet is compelled to rely on "snapshots" (rather than on a seamless narrative) to convey old age, the arrest of forward motion,
and the dwindling of memory's treasured images. His poems
need to mimic weakness, immobility, and mental starvation.
But— because old age is above all retrospective, the poems
must be large enough to encompass, even if in brief memories,
the poet's life from childhood to anticipated death; and large
enough, too, to foresee what Lowell calls, in a poem about himself and his friend Peter Taylor, "our afterlife." Lowell must
combine meagerness with memorial extension and—without
repudiating his adjectival style of writing—bend his expression
to stinted models, reproducing the deletions of time. As he
takes his last look at origins and circumstance, he must coordi-

nate his present with his past and affirm, with binocular comprehension, the simultaneous coexistence in late life of Eros and Thanatos.

As I have mentioned, Lowell here writes in a more interrupted style of glimpses, and he contrives multiple images of subtraction. Often these two modes are combined, and although they are separately not without parallel in his earlier poetry, it is in *Day by Day* that they become closely allied and dominant. Lowell, an only child, had by now lost to death his grandparents, his parents, and his aunts, as well as many friends and fellow writers; he had lost to manic-depressive illness the possibility of a normal life; he had lost two wives to divorce; and by leaving the United States behind, he had lost daily life in New York with Elizabeth Hardwick and their daughter, Harriet. Now, through the attrition of mutual illness (his breakdowns, Caroline's alcoholism), he was losing his third wife (and with her, daily life with his young son, Sheridan); and finally, he had lost physical strength and stamina to congestive heart disease. It is no wonder that subtraction should dominate his imagination, nor that making a final accounting, taking a last look, should lead him to a literal ledger keeping.

Subtractive literality was not, as I've said, characteristic of Lowell's past work. If we want the poet's own definition of his earlier poetic method, we can find it in the painful *Day by Day* poem "Unwanted" (which returns further back in time than any other poem in the book, to a Robert Lowell as yet unborn, unwillingly carried by a mother who did not want a child). In the past, he tells us, he used stylistic indirection—evasion, misalliance—to discover revelation, encouraging imaginative vision by searching out "farfetched" images to the exclusion of realistically transcriptive ones:

> [I] had flashes when I first found
> a humor for myself in images,
> farfetched misalliance
> that made evasion a revelation.

Can this Hamlet-like method—by indirection finding out direction—suffice in the face of death? The "misalliance" that seemed charming and humorous when, by its evasion of literality, the poet could create unexpected revelation now seems disappointing; as he will say despairingly in "Epilogue" (the poem closing *Day by Day*), "All's misalliance." Allying an image to something else—a proposition, a theme—in a "farfetched" way describes the creation of metaphor—that transfer across, or "farfetching," as Hopkins would have called it, that brings two unlikely things together. Metaphor comes under suspicion at the hour of death: last wills and testaments avoid metaphor in favor of unambiguous statement. In classical rhetoric, metaphor was conventionally praised for its "aptness," its "fit," but that was not the style of metaphor that Lowell had favored in his earlier work; there, he used metaphor to shock, to unsettle, to unnerve, to evade the collocation that would strike the reader as confirming a reliable sense of the object of comparison. The English poet Michael Hofmann, in a review of Lowell's *Collected Poems*, brilliantly described the effect of Lowell's original startling conjunctions:

> There is a sort of doubling: the more the words work
> at their mimetic tasks, the more they show themselves as
> words. . . . There is something quasi-autonomous about
> this peculiar function; it can only be done in words, but
> words handled—or purposely mishandled . . . in such a
> way that they feel physically solid, as they cannon into
> each other.[3]

In such verbal cannoning and its consequent stylistic friction, Lowell found the energy and pressure that corresponded to his notion of history in full forward overdrive. When he begins *Day by Day*, Lowell hardly knows whether to preserve his native "farfetched" style or to abjure it. Can he sustain the concentration and symbolic meaning attained by that former aggressive style of metaphor, or must he—as he seems to feel in the poem "Shifting Colors"—let his writing weaken toward the literal? To his own surprise, he finds himself uttering a plea to be spared the intensity of sense memory that stimulates metaphorical revelation:

> I seek leave unimpassioned by my body,
> I am too weak to strain to remember, or give
> recollection the eye of a microscope. I see
> horse and meadow, duck and pond,
> universal consolatory
> description without significance,
> transcribed verbatim by my eye.

And yet to "transcribe verbatim"—to say "horse and meadow, duck and pond" without the obliquity and collision of metaphor—is not truly possible for anyone who still wishes, as Lowell does, to imagine images and compose poetry. My aim in what follows is to trace, through Lowell's images and statements of literal subtraction, how *Day by Day* takes its last look and remains—while conveying the weakness, stasis, and emotional starvation of age—imaginatively alive, on the side of creativity. We need to take note of Lowell's single subtractions, but also to ask how they are arranged (or, as Elizabeth Bishop would say in her elegy for Lowell, "deranged"). The judgment voiced in "deranged" sprang to Bishop's mind not only from Lowell's handling of his recent sonnets (cannibalized from the volume called *Notebook* and re-formed into the volumes called *History* and *For Lizzie and Harriet*) but also, probably, from a first reading of *Day by Day*. Much of the poetry of *Day by Day* evades logic, or "deranges" sequence. I believe the "derangement" is provoked by the acute need to reproduce the chiaroscuro of repeated loss and to forecast the unimaginable loss to come.

In the poem called "Our Afterlife II," for instance, Lowell writes, as Plath had done, as if he were already dead and could see himself "from the outside." He becomes the coffined corpse awaited in Boston's Church of the Advent, from which (in obedience to his legal will) he was to be buried. Death's subtractions appear here in the present tense, not the future, as Lowell watches his contemporaries die:

> The old boys drop like wasps
> from windowsill and pane.
> In a church
> the Psalmist's glass mosaic shepherd
> and bright green pastures
> seem to wait
> with the modish faithlessness
> and erotic daydream
> of art nouveau for our funeral.

The poet's arresting move here is to treat the stained-glass window's literal religious matter—the shepherd of the twenty-third Psalm allegorically representing Jesus—in a distancing manner denoting his loss of faith. With faith subtracted, the poet can register only the window's aesthetic style—secular, erotic, modish. There is no "farfetched" metaphor here, no evasion of the literal matter of the church window. What is Lowellesque is the way in which facts of matter and facts of manner are blasphemously fused as word succeeds word. Words of re-

77

ligious import—"church" and "Psalmist" and "shepherd" and "green pastures"—attract each other because they belong to a single semiotic field; and even imagining that the Shepherd of souls would "wait" as the poet enters the valley of the shadow of death would not violate religious sentiment. But to every religious word here some connoisseur's word has been attached. Lowell mentions the material appearance of the Shepherd as "glass mosaic" and comments on the glassmaker's particular choice of "bright" green for the representation of the green pastures. Whereas the true Shepherd would indeed "wait" for the dying believer, this stained-glass Jesus, being an aesthetic construct, merely "seems" to wait. Where faith should be, there is the faithlessness of fashionable art, art of a "modish" sort commissioned for the church's turn-of-the-century "up-to-date" windows. Where contemplation should be, the sensuous power of the art-nouveau style introduces instead an "erotic daydream"; and with eternity subtracted from his view, the poet can merely notice, name, and judge the aesthetic deficiencies, for a divine subject, of the too-fashionable art nouveau.

What are we to make of Lowell's aesthetic "pollution" of his Christian stained-glass window? And how are we to react to Lowell's apparent callousness of reference to "the old boys" who "drop like wasps" from their own, different, windowpane? The deletion of self that is effected by such a strategy is total: the poet is nothing more than another unregretted wasp; his funeral will be attended only by the surrounding church decorations, not by his Savior. By interleaving the sacred nouns of religion with estimating words of connoisseurship, Lowell, after inviting into the poem the moment of cultural belief in which the window was installed in good faith, "corrects" that belief as if he were a secular art historian so alienated from an ongoing funeral service that he is reduced to judging the church appointments. The pang that ought to attend the phrase "our funeral" is held off in favor of a detachment marked by the semi-blasphemous *frisson* attending the mixed diction that assimilates wasps to men, the Good Shepherd to modish art. There is indeed a brief resort to metaphor in the subtracted wasps, but the rest is literal: the poet himself, about to be subtracted, is unmetaphorically real, the stained glass with faith subtracted is merely real, and Lowell's silent subtraction of the psalmist's earnest "for Thou art with me" into a feigned semblance of waiting is a denatured "real."

The detached and literal manner of "Our Afterlife II" affects images throughout *Day by Day*, especially those conveying the physical state of the aging body. Not only do such images minimize metaphor, they are also voiced in a "low" diagnostic diction of bruises and bumps unsuitable for the "revelation" aimed at by the earlier "misalliances" of metaphor:

> Our mannerisms harden—
> a bruise is immortal,
> the instant egg on my shin
> I got from braking a car
> too sharply a year ago
> stays firm brown and yellow,
> the all-weather color for death.

Could any respectable poetry be closer to transcriptive prose? Except for the mention of "hardened" mannerisms, a single whimsical exaggeration—"a bruise is immortal," and the "dead" metaphor of the egg bump—the passage could come from anyone's diary. Other passages about bodily decline take on greater drama but remain literal, as in the uttering of Lowell's fear of the gross physical subtractions of accidental death and his dread of prolonged pain:

> I ask for a natural death,
> no teeth on the ground,
> no blood about the place . . .
> It's not death I fear,
> but unspecified, unlimited pain.

Yet another such literal moment looks to a futile future, imagining the most literal subtraction of all, as the body becomes a corpse:

> the time when any illness is chronic,
> and the years of discretion are spent on complaint—
>
> until the wristwatch is taken from the wrist.

The close of that passage exemplifies the factuality of which I have been speaking, but it also reveals yet again Lowell's subtractive way of managing images into meagerness, done here with peculiar exactness: take the word "wristwatch" (the poet says), subtract "watch" (as the hospital attendant will do after death), and the despoiled naked "wrist" is left unadorned and time-less, exposed, dead.

Subtraction is all the more conspicuous in late Lowell because his poetic aim has so often, in the past, been one of accumulation. Critics pointed out, when Lowell appeared on the scene, his heavy artillery of adjectives and nouns, volleys of them, noisily "cannoning"—to return to Hofmann's verb—across the page. The rhetorical antagonist of this former accumulation, the managing of subtraction, is in *Day by Day* equally exhilarating to watch, though it is often, on the page, eerie to encounter—most eerie, perhaps, when Lowell subtracts himself from himself, stopping the poem cold. At the end of his elegy to his mother, he says—and we at first feel we are hearing from the poet the recommended "mature" understanding of a difficult parent—

> It has taken me the time since you died
> to discover you are as human as I am. . . .

Chillingly, Lowell appends a closing self-deleting proviso—"If I am." Earlier, he had been Caligula, Medusa, a monster: "Pity the monsters!" he had cried, being one of them. Uncertain, as he leaves the stage, whether he has at last metamorphosed into a human being, he stops and subtracts himself, by his final hypothesis, from the human species.

A more gruesome self-subtractive closure appears in the poem called "Turtle." It begins with an anecdote: as a boy, Lowell had tried to pick up a snapping turtle by what he thought was the tail but was in reality a foreleg. "I could have lost a finger," he says wryly, with adult detachment. The end of "Turtle," however, unrolls a grisly reprise in nightmare of the child's original fear. Many other life events have died, in the unrolling of the reel of accumulated memory, but not this one of mutilating amputation:

> Too many pictures
> have screamed from the reel . . . in the rerun,
> the snapper holds on till sunset—
> in the awful instantness of retrospect,
> its beak
> works me underwater drowning by my neck,
> as it claws away pieces of my flesh
> to make me small enough to swallow.

The transmutation of the literality of dream into aesthetic patterning is accomplished here by the presence of sonic echo and parallel syntax: "awful" phonetically matches "claws" and "swallow"; "retrospect" harshly prophesies "beak" and "works" and "neck" and "make." The original "farfetched" cinematic metaphor of recursive extended time, "the rerun," is corrected by the poet's remarking on the dream's "awful instantness of retrospect." The turtle's piece-by-piece clawing and swallowing take place within the dream instantaneously, as the nightmare mimics the assaultive simultaneity of images on Lowell's old-age screen, presenting and subtracting at the same moment.

In another mood, Lowell keeps the horror of death's subtraction at arm's length by a humor that transmutes subtraction into more congenial (or comic) figures of loss, either a decrease in weight or (by deletion of time) a decrease in age. As Lowell, now divorced, visits Elizabeth Hardwick in the New York apartment of their long marriage, the furniture seems to be becoming less heavy in a retrograde and subtractive motion that will in time ensure its complete disappearance:

> I can give the dates when they entered our lives:
>
> Cousin Belle's half-sofa,
> her carrot dangled before famished heirs,
> is twenty years lighter.
>
> The small portrait of Cousin Cassie,
> corsetted like the Empress Eugénie
> and willed to father when I was seven,
> is now too young for me to talk to.

As furniture becomes lighter and portraits younger in their asymptotic approaches to nothingness, Lowell himself, in inverse proportion, grows burdened and older. As he arrives at death, these life-long objects will reach ultimate weightlessness and vanish with him.

As one becomes conscious of Lowell's insistence on manifesting by images the subtractions he faces, one sees them on almost every page, in every day, of *Day by Day*. Myth itself loses its solidity: Ulysses on Circe's island, after the glamour of the enchantress has faded in debasement, "dislikes everything in his impoverished life of myth." As Lowell's last walk with his third wife ends, even nostalgia for the marriage proves as temporary as the snow of yesterday; both are subtracted from the day, nostalgia by violent mental destruction, snow by its nature as a transient thing: "nostalgia pulverized by thought, / nomadic as yesterday's whirling snow." "Les neiges d'antan," originally metaphorical, have been literalized into real weather, "yesterday's ... snow." Anything that *can* be subtracted from living—from nostalgia to snow to the human body to the idealizations of myth—will, somewhere in these pages, *be* subtracted.

There are, in the longer poems of *Day by Day*, more complex portrayals of old age, in which the subtractions that have already happened, and are only too evident to others, are denied by the self in a vain attempt to sustain the hallucination of one's continued youth. One of Lowell's surrogate selves—an old wine baron in the poem "Ear of Corn"—acts out this delusion of persistent youth as he insists on seeing himself as sexually powerful still. At a dinner party, the baron becomes, to Lowell, a horrifying image of himself, an aged Pluto who wants to carry off a young Persephone (daughter of the corn goddess, Demeter, hence the title "Ear of Corn"). In the central passage of the poem, at table, the old host bends his sexual attention on a guest's young wife, who looks back at him, disgusted:

> His eyes never leave her lips.
> She cannot cure his hallucination
> he can bribe or stare
> any woman he wants into orgasm. . . .
> He fills her ear
> with his old sexual gramophone.
> . . . .
> Her face is delicate and disgusted,
> as if she had been robbed, raped,
> or repudiated by her mother.

For his conclusion to "Ear of Corn," Lowell borrows from Saint Paul's epigram in Hebrews: "Faith is the substance of things hoped for." Lowell cruelly uses the exalted biblical phrase as a summary of the delusion of youth that the spindly legged wine baron and by implication Lowell himself strive to maintain by subtracting (as they think) years from their old faces by fastening themselves to young women:

> Is this the substance hoped for,
> after a grasshopper life of profit—
> to stand shaking on fine green legs,
> to meet the second overflowing of Eros,
> himself younger in each young face . . . ?

The poem immediately corrects this self-deceiving subtraction of years in the lines following, when the old baron looks into the face of the young wife, his guest, and suddenly, in the mirror of her disgusted face, comes to see himself as he hideously is,

> [seeing] in that mirror
> a water without the life of water,
> a face aging
> to less generosity than it had.

Those characteristic words of subtraction, "without" and "less," counter the baron's false earlier subtraction of years when he saw himself "younger." Metaphoric though "Ear of Corn" sometimes is (in its parabolic grasshopper, its resort to a fertility myth), it subsides, as do so many of these *Day by Day* poems, into the literal, even if the literal becomes almost unintelligible, as in the evocation of sexual impotence in the subtractive idea of "a water without the life of water."

Although the idea that age and death subtract value is not new, what is new in Lowell's verse in *Day by Day* is not only his fertility in finding a plethora of words and images for subtraction, but also his use of subtraction as a major rhetorical move, as in the diptych and closing summary of "Ear of Corn." But, we might ask, can Lowell not counter that idea of age's successive subtractions by an account of what age is said to add to life—the wisdom associated with experience, perhaps, or that "second overflowing of Eros" celebrated in *The Dolphin* and prolonged in the poems about Caroline and Sheridan in *Day by Day*? It seems he cannot; in *Day by Day* even affirmative poems end in loss. "Marriage," for instance, at first presents itself as the most confident love poem in the volume but is shaken as it progresses. On the left panel (Part I) of this marriage diptych, we see the new Lowell family group: the poet himself, Caroline (already pregnant with Sheridan), and Caroline's three daughters from a former marriage, all dressed in "Sunday-best" for what Lowell calls, with ironic alliteration, "the formal family photograph in color." The unseen "center of symmetry" in that family photograph, the poet adds, is his as-yet-unborn son. The right panel of the diptych (Part II) offers a different marriage group; we see Van Eyck's "formal family portrait" of the couple Giovanni and Giovanna Arnolfini:

> His wife's with child;
> he lifts a hand,
> thin and white as his face
> held up like a candle to bless her . . .
> smiling, swelling, blossoming. . . .
> . . . .
> They are rivals in homeliness and love;
> her hand lies like china in his,
> her other hand
> is in touch with the head of her unborn child.
> They wait and pray,
> as if the airs of heaven

that blew on them when they married
were now a common visitation.

But that gentle portrait of marriage, and that prayer for the continued favor of the airs of heaven, are undone by the end of the poem, which at first returns us to the merely momentary flash of the contemporary photographer, and then tells us that Giovanni will die twenty years before Giovanna—as though one figure in the Arnolfini portrait were suddenly subtracted by erasure. Lowell's flash-forward prophesies his own end:

> They wait and pray,
> as if the airs of heaven
> that blew on them when they married
> were now a common visitation,
> not a miracle of lighting
> for the photographer's sacramental instant.
>
> Giovanni and Giovanna,
> who will outlive him by 20 years . . .

By reducing the sacrament of marriage—with its promise of fidelity unto death—to "the photographer's sacramental instant," Lowell deletes all binding promise beyond the instant of the camera flash; and by deleting Giovanni from the couple in the portrait, he deletes Giovanna's naive trust in the perpetuity of heaven's blessing. Just as "Last Walk?" had ended with the pulverization of nostalgia by thought, so "Marriage"—after its comparison of a contemporary family photograph to a Renaissance family portrait—defaces both pictures by subtraction, unable to leave them in the original mode of prayer and promise.

But surely, we say, resisting Lowell's unhappy last looks, age exhibits something additive, something that is not waning? Is there, in Lowell, no binocular view of an aliveness cohabiting with deadness? Perhaps, no matter how the body fails, the mental realm is immune to subtractions? We are rewarded by seeing how Lowell, in a striking poem addressed to his old friend Peter Taylor, allows for the improvement in art made possible by the accretion of years. The title itself, however, introduces death as the price exacted for that ripened art: the poem is called "Our Afterlife I." It exemplifies, in its series of images darting from present to past, from possessor to inheritor, from Taylor's Tennessee to Lowell's England, the poet's "deranged" way of conducting his last poems, glance by glance. Here, the initial glimpse is a buoyant one of two birds, sketched—as we might by now expect—in literal image followed by literal personal statement. Lowell observes two red cardinals who "dart and tag and mate— / young as they want to be"—as he and Peter Taylor are not:

> Southbound—
> a couple in passage,
> two Tennessee cardinals
> in green December outside the window
> dart and tag and mate—
> young as they want to be.
> We're not.
> Since my second fatherhood
> and stay in England, I am a generation older.

Yet Lowell and Taylor, even if threatened by the infirmities of age, can be assimilated to the free and sexual cardinals, or so the poet tries to think:

> We are dangerously happy—
> our book-bled faces
> streak like red birds,
> dart unstably, ears cocked to catch
> the first shy whisper of deafness.

87

However, a single loss, that of hearing, once mentioned, generates violent subtractions, Time's recent "killings" of fellow writers:

> This year killed
> Pound, Wilson, Auden....

Forced by these deaths to acknowledge his own mortality, Lowell fears the loss of the bloom of vigor in himself and his friend, themselves once promising beginners. Now, in age, they are jealous of the young "inheritors" biding their time, waiting for the patriarchs to die:

> promise has lost its bloom,
> the inheritor reddens
> like a false rose—
> nodding, nodding, nodding.

The poet recalls the time "when Cupid"—he of the emblematically red hearts—"was still the Christ of love's religion," and time seemed—with "sleight of hand"—to stand still. Besieged by the cold wave outside and the tinnitus ringing in his ear inside, aware of the stealthy advance of the clock, the poet declares in an aphorism the paradoxical additive subtractions of the end of life: "Each saving breath / takes something."

Against the melancholy conclusion that subtraction is the single constant quality of his present life, Lowell rises to a memorable defense of age's contribution to art. If the young inheritor knew the cost of life, he would not envy the aging writer. Nonetheless, in spite of all the subtractions, old writers, like old painters, are rich in their accumulation of perspectives as they stand on the eminence of experience and expertise:

> This is riches:
> the eminence not to be envied,

> the account
> accumulating layer and angle,
> face and profile,
> 50 years of snapshots,
> the ladder of ripening likeness.

After fifty years, the painter has accumulated a comprehensive album of sketches recording layer and angle, face and profile; the photographer, though he has only an instant for his flash, can point to his full portfolio of snapshots; the aspiring poet has at last reached the height of metaphor by ascending his Frostian "ladder of ripening likeness." Now he can pluck the mature fruit of his labors—what Frost (in "After Apple-picking") called "the great harvest I myself desired."

With the Keatsian "ripening" of the fruit of imagination, an implied redness returns to suffuse the poem, and for a moment Lowell and Taylor can once again be the darting birds of aliveness. Perhaps recollecting Heidegger's "thrownness"—the fact that we find ourselves pitched into existence without any choice in the matter—the poet depicts the still-airborne selves of himself and his friend:

> We are things thrown in the air
> alive in flight. . . .

Had the poem ended there, it would have announced a victory over death, its last image a triumphant one of soaring aliveness. But even this—the most affirmative poem in *Day by Day*—has to admit the truth: that (to adapt Frost) nothing red can stay. The ripening declines into rust; but with a second reactive claim for life, Lowell turns back to a different Keatsian image, that of the "chameleon poet." If the red vitality of the poet and his friend has faded over time to rust, it is because as artists, still alive, they are taking on, as always, the color of their context:

> We are things thrown in the air
> alive in flight . . .
> our rust the color of the chameleon.

The subtraction of redness has now become an advantage, adding another color, layer, and angle to the creations of old age. The balance of subtraction and addition in "Our Afterlife I" seems to me the most finely achieved structure in *Day by Day*, false neither to subtraction nor to addition. Its "thinking in images" bears witness to a process of thought that begins in the warmth of life-long friendship, mentions present infirmities, musters the riches of experience as advantage, reiterates the aliveness of the friends' mental and physical being, but in the end admits age's subtraction of color and energy, turning red to rust, while contradicting that subtraction by affirming the artist's still-transformative power to change, chameleon-like, with circumstance.

There is then a consoling aesthetic advantage in the productions of age; the later snapshots in the accomplished photographer's album are bound to surpass the early "blunders" that Lowell recalls in the poem "Suicide":

> . . . our first home-photographs,
> headless, half-headed, tilting
> extinguished by a flashbulb.

Even so, *Day by Day*'s defense of experience as a perfecting of art cannot reach the gladness of "Fishnet," Lowell's earlier account of vocation in *The Dolphin*:

> Yet my heart rises, I know I've gladdened a lifetime
> knotting, undoing a fishnet of tarred rope;
> the net will hang on the wall when the fish are eaten,
> nailed like illegible bronze on the futureless future.[4]

Yet even that passage, invoking the *aere perennius* of Horace's claim, must end with subtraction, as Lowell acknowledges that since his art—like all art—will eventually lose cultural intelligibility, it can have no permanent future. But the dactyls of the quatrain ring nonetheless with triumph, not submission: the poet's net of forms in *The Dolphin* will remain, in his hammered phrase, "nailed like illegible bronze on the futureless future."

The later volume *Day by Day*, in its elegiac last looks at life, cannot make its claims for the future in such a Roman tone. At most, it looks to a new generation to better its own accomplishments. In "For Sheridan," the most moving poem of binocular vision in *Day by Day*, Lowell takes as his subject the uncanny resemblance of his son at five to a photograph of himself at five. The inner blindness of his own life, the result of past biological and psychic damage, is subsumed in the childlike word "hurt." Alluding to Saint Paul's "For we see now through a glass darkly," he identifies his early self, before he was damaged, with the self of his young son:

> We could see clearly
> and all the same things
> before the glass was hurt.

This poem of almost disbelieving hope ends with the poet's crushing recollection of his own intentions and failures, coupled with a wish for a better life for Sheridan. It ends in a standoff between the subtractive failures of Lowell's own life and a hope for Sheridan's future. Lowell tips the scales toward hope by ending on the additive word "better":

> Past fifty, we learn with surprise and a sense
> of suicidal absolution
> that what we intended and failed

could never have happened—
and must be done better.

Lowell—as he is always likely to do in *Day by Day*—returns to
literal statement here, depending for emotional effect on the
allusion to the "hurt" that made him unable to carry out his
own life intentions. Because he does not want Sheridan to
come to his own point of helpless "suicidal absolution," he insists, though in an impersonal form, that Sheridan must carry
out the intentions of his own life better than his father has
done. "Better"—the comparative of improvement—echoes
into vacancy, as Lowell, "suicidally" absolving himself, subtracts
himself from the field of action, leaving it to his son. At least,
Lowell reflects, the scene of the world has been repopulated in
the person of this child, who brings the same Lowellesque
physical features, but perhaps a healthier, or more normal,
psyche, to the endeavors of life. The old year disappears, the
new youthful one comes forth from the wings, and Lowell's
journal, *Day by Day*, ends as we might have anticipated, on actual fact, as the poet adds his son to the sum of things while
subtracting his own life as unsalvageable.

When Wallace Stevens's friend Henry Church died, the
poet wrote of Sleep and Peace as figures in the "mythology of
modern death" ("The Owl in the Sarcophagus"). Those alle-
gorical personages, though secularized, bore a strong resemblance to Christian images of death, as Stevens's rhythms bore
resemblance both to lullaby and to hymn. The enormous difference in tone between Stevens's ornate murmuring farewells
and Lowell's acute and worldly images—an art-nouveau
church window, a nightmare of being swallowed alive, Cousin
Belle's sofa, cardinals in flight, a family photograph—testifies
to the major change in the elegiac vocabulary of American po-

etry brought about by Robert Lowell, who, with his subtractions and his literalness, gave a spare and contemporary tone,
in *Day by Day*, to the confrontation of mental energy and
physical decline.

Caught and Freed: Elizabeth Bishop and *Geography III*

Elizabeth Bishop's last published book, the 1976 *Geography III*, was not composed in any knowledge of certain death; Bishop died suddenly, two years after the appearance of that collection, at sixty-eight. Nonetheless, she was writing several of its poems—and other poems composed after its publication, to be included here—with approaching death in mind. My title "Caught and Freed" in fact comes from one such poem, called "Sonnet," concerning the moment when the poet, after death, becomes her poems. I begin, however, with a failed poem, the 1974 "Breakfast Song," from a recent edition containing Bishop's manuscript drafts that were never released by Bishop for publication.[1] This unsatisfactory poem (addressed to the young woman who was Bishop's partner) illustrates baldly (and therefore very clearly) the difficulty of the attempt to take a steady and comprehensive view of emotional life and repellent death within a single poem. The twenty-two lines of "Breakfast Song" cannot find an adequate binocular vision; in fact, they do their utmost to keep the picturing of ugly death separate from the picturing of erotic life. The six opening lines and three closing lines, serving as brackets, present life undisturbed by the idea of dying, but the middle of the poem offers a grisly view of the poet's future burial in which all warmth will be lost:

My love, my saving grace,
your eyes are awfully blue.
I kiss your funny face,
your coffee-flavored mouth.
Last night I slept with you.
Today I love you so
how can I bear to go
(as soon I must, I know)
to bed with ugly death
in that cold, filthy place,
to sleep there without you,
without the easy breath
and nightlong, limblong warmth
I've grown accustomed to?
—Nobody wants to die;
tell me it is a lie!
But no, I know it's true.
It's just the common case;
there's nothing one can do.
My love, my saving grace,
Your eyes are awfully blue
early and instant blue.

The closing reprise of life does not mention, as the opening did, the funny face or the coffee-flavored mouth or even the past night's warmth, because it wishes to sequester all of life's meaning in a pair of blue eyes—"awfully blue / early and instant blue." The eyes' intensity, their dawn-earliness, and their instant blue *are* life. What the poet sees in the beloved's eyes is freshness, readiness, quickness of response.

So what is wrong with this piece of verse? It looks with its right eye, and it sees blue; it looks with its left eye, and it sees filth. The two elements, life and death, can muster no arc of resemblance bringing them together as experiences of a single sensibility. The speaker is struck by the beauty and warmth of love; then she fears being mated with the cold and ugly stranger, Death. Her recoil from her look at "ugly death" returns her to the blue eyes in an amnesiac way; the last three lines, unable to integrate the two looks, affect not to remember—as they immerse themselves in the blue of the saving grace—the vision of the sordid grave. Willed amnesia is not, in the end, a valid recourse for an imaginative mind. And there is another drawback: the bedding down with Death in "that cold, filthy place" resonates more intensely in the mind of the reader than do the blue eyes.

By contrast, the light-winged poem called "Sonnet,"[2] composed too late for inclusion in *Geography III*, is successful in holding death and life in a single conceptual frame, that of inorganic objects. Although it gestures to the form of the sonnet in its fourteen lines, it also jests with that form by turning its divisions upside down and altering its breadth. In Bishop's "sonnet," the sestet precedes the octave rather than the octave the sestet,[3] and its lines are merely two beats wide (in lieu of the true sonnet's five-beat width):

> Caught—the bubble
> in the spirit-level,
> a creature divided;
> and the compass needle
> wobbling and wavering,
> undecided.
> Freed—the broken
> thermometer's mercury
> running away;
> and the rainbow-bird

from the narrow bevel
of the empty mirror,
flying wherever
it feels like, gay!

Sestet and octave in "Sonnet" are not separated by white space but are distinguished by syntactic means: each occupies a single sentence. The sestet sentence, opening with the word "Caught," introduces (as symbols of the body) two inorganic devices of exact measurement—a spirit-level and a compass, whereas the octave sentence, beginning with the word "Freed," displays *its* instrument of exact measurement—a thermometer—as already broken. Bishop turns away from such fastidious exactness of measurement with her closing image of a sun-generated "rainbow-bird" flashing its spectrum here and there from the beveled edge of a mirror, just as her spirit, after death, will flash from the shaped edges of poems that mirror her world.

There is an architectural solidity to this poem, as it divides personhood into a period during which it is caught, and a second period—with a longer number of lines—when it is freed. Although these periods of imprisonment and liberty are clearly distinguished by their first words, "Caught" and "Freed," they are united as manifestations of a single sensibility by their grammatically parallel present participles—"wobbling" and "wavering" in the first state, "running" and "flying" in the second. These reveal that the "creature" being observed has not changed, in its transition, its active manner of action but merely the nature of that action. Nor has the spirit creature (the bubble of the level, the needle of the compass) changed, in its freed state, its "genetic code" as the determining element of an instrument of measurement: in our first sight of its freed state as mercury, it is still derived from its measuring instrument, a thermometer. The long, narrow shape of the level, the compass needle, and the thermometer is retained in the bevel from which the "rainbow-bird" springs. There is wit in this poem: its feelings have found for themselves unexpected correlatives that parallel, but do not repeat, religious images of the spirit caught in the body, of the erring and unresolved will, and of the conscience's regulation of temperance (here altered to temperature). Just as the image of the bubble caught in the spirit-level echoes old images of the soul as a dewdrop, so the image of the undecided compass needle, recalling the erring human will, sums up Bishop's vacillations between North and South, Nova Scotia and Brazil, her "questions of travel."

Supplied with her refurbished religious emblems of imprisonment and freedom—"Who shall deliver me from the body of this death?"—Bishop must decide on her stance toward her material. She chooses not to enter the lyric *in propria persona*— there is no "I" here—but rather elects a stance of objectivity, that of an impartial observer who can view, disinterestedly, the antithetical states of being caught and being freed. An observer capable of this degree of impartiality, in a religious poem, would be God or a devout speaker, judging the spirit happier in its freed state than in its captivity within the body. But Bishop's poem will not impersonate God and will not introduce the speaker as a Christian believer. On the contrary: Bishop's poem is scientific not only in its symbolic use of instruments of precise measurement but also in its impersonal knowledge of the two states it analyzes, "caught" and "freed," presenting them as a chemist might present alternative states of water as ice and steam. The divided and undecided creature of the first state is still as "mercurial" as ever in the second state—but now the mercury runs free, once the thermometer, broken, need no longer monitor the spirit's intemperance: "A broken and a contrite heart, O God, thou wilt not despise" (Psalm 51). And Bishop's final mirror is still a mirror, capable of accurate (if reversed) representation, though it now lacks a person standing before its judging eye; empty, it need not reflect a particular image color from the available spectrum but can let its whole inner being flash free from its beveled edge, flying "wherever / it feels like." The gaiety celebrated in the last word is never available untroubled during life, when the spirit is still "fettered in feet, and manacled with hands" (Marvell). Yet an aura of precision remains: if the mirror were not beveled, shaped with an exactly calibrated edge, it could not generate the "rainbow-bird." The spirit "level" has been transformed into a rhyming mirror-"bevel," subsuming once again the first caught state and the final freed one under a single arc.

Unlike "Breakfast Song," "Sonnet" does not inflict a "hard" conceptual separation on life and death: the bubble can move around in the spirit-level until it finds its harmonious center; the compass needle can take various positions until it stops at its true north; the mercury can live in and out of the thermometer. And Bishop does not entirely oppose life and death but fuses the two halves of her poem by inserting in both, as we have seen, metaphors of instrumentation, participles of voluntary activity, and matching rhymes. In "Breakfast Song," life was organic and warm, death inorganic and cold; in "Sonnet," the inorganic bubble and needle, mercury and mirror, undergo— as the poet at her death becomes her poems—a graceful metamorphosis into an image combining the inorganic with the organic—a "rainbow-bird." In Bishop's poem "Insomnia," the moon sought "a mirror in which to dwell," a mirror now transformed into the dwelling place of the rainbow-bird, who is liberated when the straight bevel interacts with the white light invisibly bearing within itself the multicolored spectrum.[4] (The "rainbow, rainbow, rainbow" of Bishop's freed fish finds an echo here.)

And whereas the trimeters of "Breakfast Song" have no marked representational function, the slender dimeters of "Sonnet" mimic the fine rectangular shapes, horizontal and vertical, of Bishop's related images—the spirit-level, the compass needle, the thermometer, and even the bevel. In their lightness of rhythmic motion, the dimeters help to release the confined spirit. The rhyming of two symbols within each part—as the "creature divided" rhymes with the "needle . . . undecided," and the mercury running "away" rhymes with the rainbowbird, "gay"—makes the sonnet a four-part poem—symbol-symbol, symbol-symbol—as well as a two-part one of sestet and octave. By these similar patterns of rhyming, the caught body and the freed spirit are made to resemble, and to be congruent with, each other. Bishop's imagining of the human being, in "Sonnet," has room within it for processes of both living and dying and for the tension between them, as well as for the weary desire for freedom from the body. The speaker, it is clear, feels straitened by the body and impatient of the will's life-long wavering. But instead of emphasizing the confinement and fatigue of the aged state, the poem imagines its opposite—the exhilaration of liberty, the turn from tragedy or stoicism to an envisioned brilliance of being.

The pressure of death within life makes itself felt in Bishop's last overtly elegiac poems, especially in her elegy "North Haven," written after the death in 1977 of her close friend and fellow poet Robert Lowell. And will this late poem, like "Breakfast Song," establish a "hard" division between life and death, or will it, like "Sonnet," find a way to unite them within a binocular view? Although Bishop's elegy for Lowell warns us (with its epigraph *"In memoriam: Robert Lowell"*) that it is an elegy, it "pretends" during its first four stanzas that it is not one. Rather, it occupies itself at first with defining life as pure sense perception, apparently untroubled by temporality. I'll come in a moment to the final stanzas, but I will begin with the first four.

Simple perception is always momentary, a brief bodily registering. "North Haven" opens with a stanza of such perception, recording nothing more than a boat on the water, new cones on the spruce trees, the quiet appearance of the bay, and a single cloud in the sky. Living, in this prelude, is indistinguishable from seeing and describing: change, though implied in the "new" evergreen cones, is not central to it. Setting off this moment of pure perception by italicizing it, Bishop intimates a sense of homecoming and pleasure in her seasonal return to the island of North Haven (off the coast of Maine, in Penobscot Bay). Is this vista not enough (the poet asks by her repeated auxiliary "can") by which to characterize the state of being alive?

> *I can make out the rigging of a schooner*
> *a mile off; I can count*
> *the new cones on the spruce. It is so still*
> *the pale bay wears a milky skin, the sky*
> *no clouds, except for one long, carded horse's-tail.*

When the poem resumes, the speaker allows time to enter briefly, but undisturbingly, allowing us to know that she was here "last summer." She continues the joyous inventory of her surroundings and remarks on her responses to them, realistic and imaginative: "The islands haven't shifted since last summer, / Even if I like to pretend they have." It is true that a glancing sense of another person or persons enters half concealed in the word "our" in stanza three—"This month our favorite [island] is full of flowers"—but the pronoun is faint beside the delighted catalog of the blossoming species the poet sees, all of them familiar, all of them "returned" (like herself) and bent to

101

a single purpose, "to paint the meadows with delight." Perception continues with further abundantly collective specification, reproducing last summer's field of flowers in today's identical one, amassing a plenitude of flower names (capitalized as if in a seed catalogue) with allusions to flower-loving fellow poets (Shakespeare, Marianne Moore):

> Buttercups, Red Clover, Purple Vetch,
> Hawkweed still burning, Daisies pied, Eyebright,
> the Fragrant Bedstraw's incandescent stars,
> and more, returned, to paint the meadows with delight.[5]

In stanza four, Bishop inserts the first disturbing note of the poem as she attempts to repeat her recognition of the perennial flowers by announcing the return of the "same" birds (adding the sense of hearing to a poem hitherto restricted to sight while retaining the continued emphasis on pure sense perception). But if the daisies seem identical to those of last year, the birds, the poet admits, may or may not be so. Bishop denies them the species immortality of Keats's nightingale: "Thou wast not born for death, immortal bird!" Rather, Bishop questions Keats's certainty: "The Goldfinches are back, or others like them.... / Nature repeats herself, or almost does." The "or's" are concessives; perhaps these are different species of finches; maybe the sparrows' song—which the poet thinks she recognizes—has been altered. For the moment, she tries to insist, by specifying its five-note character, that the song is still the same:

> The Goldfinches are back, or others like them,
> and the white-throated Sparrow's five-note song,
> pleading and pleading, brings tears to the eyes.

These tears are the tears of elegy, hitherto suppressed in Bishop's insistence on remaining within the timeless precincts of perception, as she maintains her intense desire to keep the island untainted by death. The poet has wished to see her island impervious to change, but the death of her friend has been hovering underneath all her grateful recognitions of returned flowers and recognized birds. Lowell's death has been threatening to occupy Bishop's consciousness and is, I think, responsible for the way she makes each stanza of perception and warm naming slow down at the close, as if unwilling to move forward. The last line of each stanza of the poem is always a retarding hexameter, unexpected after the preceding (mostly) pentameter lines.[6] Now the hitherto-suppressed death, "hiding" in these reluctant hexameters, is about to come forcibly into view.

At the close of the fourth stanza, Bishop voices the distinction, central to the poem, between the recursive action of cyclical nature (to repeat) and the voluntary action of perfection-seeking writers (to revise). Yet the poet bafflingly juxtaposes the two verbs, one impersonal, one human, in an italicized line:

> Nature repeats herself, or almost does:
> *Repeat, repeat, repeat; revise, revise, revise.*

This onomatopoeic line imitates birdsong, its first half echoing (in the spelling and long "e" of "repeats") the "pleading and pleading" of the sparrow, replicating Nature's predictability: *plead, plead, plead; repeat, repeat, repeat.* But what of the second half of the line? It makes a new triple "birdsong," but makes it out of a "human" word, "revise," which, like Lowell's death, has been waiting under the surface of the poem. For the moment, its surprising intellectual appearance, immediately following the repeating perceptual birdsong, remains an unaccountable one.

The presence of the dead friend—when Bishop makes it appear, apparently unbidden, in the speaker's resistant perceptions—introduces, against nature's comforting replications,

103

time as a non-repetitive, non-recursive presence, tapering off into loss:

> Years ago, you told me it was here
> (in 1932?) you first "discovered *girls*"
> and learned to sail, and learned to kiss.
> You had "such fun," you said, that classic summer.
> ("Fun"—it always seemed to leave you at a loss. . . .)

Because it is normal, in writing elegy, to mention early in the poem the death occasioning it, Bishop's postponement of the arrival of the other, shadowy half of the early "we" (which generated the mention of "our" island) is unsettling. We are puzzled to find the poet's friend lamented so late, and in such apparently banal fashion, being quoted as having, on this island, "'discovered *girls*' / and learned to sail, and learned to kiss." The island, hitherto populated (to the speaker's view) solely by flowers and birds, now takes on a new (if vanished) population of adolescents and sailing parties and romances. The island is no longer nature; it is society. The speaker can no longer greet with joy the daisies and the goldfinches; she is being forced, by memory, into social interchange and loss. The reminiscence concerning the dead friend, "Years ago, you told me," darkens, with the increasing pain of his absence, into that well-known reactive resurrective move, a direct address to the lost one. In the past, the living Lowell came to North Haven and then left, summer after summer. But those temporary departures are over, and Bishop's words must alter from the first temporary preterite—"You left"—to a permanent present-perfect parting—"you've left / for good":

> You left North Haven, anchored in its rock,
> afloat in mystic blue. . . . And now—you've left
> for good.

Every elegy must contain at least one moment in which the actual death of the lost person "happens over again," is enacted rather than merely reported. Bishop's first way of enacting the crushing loss of her closest friend has been, as we've seen, to obliterate Lowell entirely from the once-shared scene, showing her speaker attempting to fix herself in a state of pure timeless aesthetic perception. In effect, the poet almost obliterates the speaker as well, as she reduces her at first to pure eye (no other senses are permitted entrance to the first stanza). By introducing the passage of time in the first-stanza phrase "last summer"; by giving a hint of another person in the second-stanza adjective "our"; by allowing hearing, in the bird stanza, to join sight; and finally by her fourth-stanza admission of tears and the human self-correction of revision, Bishop prepares her speaker to acknowledge the ever-present absence of Lowell. He is at last permitted actual entrance to the poem as a "living person" when the speaker recalls his mention (in the past tense) of their island. The speaker herself, musing in recollection ("'Fun'—it always seemed to leave you at a loss . . .)," quietly restores herself too to full emotional personhood. She had begun as an Emersonian "transparent eyeball"; now she is a mourner ending her Lowell stanza with the human word "loss."

Bishop has enacted Lowell's death by summoning his past living presence and then making him disappear: "You left . . . you've left for good." Yet even after this final erasure of Lowell the person, Bishop presses on to ask which quality of the living Lowell would, by its absence, make her feel his death most keenly. She realizes she will miss his restless revising of his poems. "I have treated published work as manuscript," he said of his full-scale revision of *Notebook 1967–68* into an enlarged and changed volume called simply *Notebook*. And even then, he could not rest content, going on to revise and reorder the contents of *Notebook* into two separate volumes, called *For Lizzie and Harriet* and *History*. Repudiating the eighteenth-century idea of a "watchmaker God," Lowell said (in his sonnet by that name) that God could not create and then stand apart: "he loved to tinker." Lowell kept his poetic spirit alive by "tinkering" with his verse, by finding revision as exhilarating as creation. As Bishop closes her poem, she re-creates Lowell's death in her elegy not by deliberately obliterating him, as in stanza 1, not by a denial of his absence that resurrects him in speech, as in stanza 5, not by sealing his departure "for good" as in stanza 6, but rather by grieving the impossibility, in death, of his revising—for the worse or for the better—his poems:

> You can't derange, or re-arrange,
> Your poems again. (But the Sparrows can their song.)
> The words won't change again. Sad friend, you cannot
>   change.

The fade-out from the second-person "you can't" to the third-person "the words won't" dissolves the author into his unchanging page. The final sentence of the poem is Bishop's ultimate farewell to her friend and fellow poet. In the closing lines, as I have said, Bishop as speaker is no longer merely an eye or an ear; she is a reconstituted whole person. But what are the sparrows doing in Bishop's closing stanza? They have been re-arranged, in italics, from symbols of repetition—*repeat, repeat, repeat*—to symbols of revision—*revise, revise, revise*. The poet's earlier concessive "or's"—"The Goldfinches are back, or others like them"; "Nature repeats herself, or almost does"—had weakened the concept of Nature as an unchanging ritual. The "or's" now exert new power in the presence of death, Nature's greatest change. It is not only Lowell who has gone; gone as well, the poet finally admits, are the flowers and birdsongs of the past summer. We now understand better the relation of the second italicized passage of the poem to the first one, Bishop's

opening stanza: the speaker's effort to obscure death by remaining in the fixed single moment of aesthetic perception
gradually became the effort to deny loss by affirming Nature's
repetitions. Unable to maintain the deceptive comfort of repetition, Bishop makes her italicized birdsong "evolve" from *repeat*
to *revise*—although that insight about Nature's own revisions
is not elaborated until Bishop concedes at the end of the poem
that the living sparrows, unlike the dead Lowell, can change
their song.

"North Haven" attempts for some time—by its successive
tactics of willed obliteration of time, self-reduction to pure eye
or ear, the illusion of rehearing the lost voice, and a resurrective
address to the dead—to refuse the binocular vision that holds
death and life in some active relation within a single sensibility.
Such strategies of denial tell us how hard it is for a poet of ecstatic sight and musical response, such as Bishop, to keep in a
view of life entwined with death not only the cessation of beautiful sights but also the cessation of poetic voice. She has badly
wanted (as she reveals in her gradual construction of her
speaker) to confine perception to the ever-beautiful skies, wa-
ters, flowers, and birds of reliable Nature. By at last bringing
together under the single overarching word "change" Lowell's
death, Nature's birdsong, and the revising of poems, Bishop
can put Lowell to rest: "Sad friend, you cannot change." By admitting change and revision into her much-loved landscape of
North Haven, Bishop could at last balance life (seen with the
aesthetic eye as joyous, recursive, and beautiful) against death
(seen as disappearance, poetic silence, and the eventual immobility of a poem after its creator's disappearance).

A more somber effort to sustain a binocular vision is visible
in Bishop's famous villanelle "One Art." Here, the poet cannot
fall back on the delighted perception of natural beauty. The villanelle grimly describes a life punctuated by a series of losses

from the trivial to the tragic, a life devoid (as we at first think) of any compensating gain. In the fiercely compressed and darkly flippant autobiography of "One Art," Bishop loses, in succession, her only souvenir of her mother (permanently hospitalized for insanity when Bishop was five); her Brazilian houses in Persepolis, Río de Janeiro, and Ouro Preto; and her partner Lota to suicide (a death symbolized in "One Art" by the loss of realms—Brazil—and a continent—South America). But Bishop has steadily refused, she tells us, to qualify any of these severe losses as "disaster." She means to invoke the etymological meaning of the word "disaster," representing the moment when the stars themselves turn irreversibly hostile. (The word is defined in the *American Heritage Dictionary* as "an unforeseen mischance bringing with it destruction of life or property or the ruin of projects, careers, etc.") For Bishop, using the word "disaster" is conclusive, and she has so far disdained to apply this hyperbolic noun to her life's losses. Now, however, she is going to undergo, it appears, a terrible catastrophe—the loss of her young lover, the one of the joking voice and the beloved gesture. Bishop prophesies here the cessation, in old age, of the erotic life and sees erotic cessation as a symbol for the body's death, the ultimate disaster:

> The art of losing isn't hard to master;
> so many things seem filled with the intent
> to be lost that their loss is no disaster.

> Lose something every day. Accept the fluster
> of lost door keys, the hour badly spent.
> The art of losing isn't hard to master.

> Then practice losing farther, losing faster:
> places, and names, and where it was you meant
> to travel. None of these will bring disaster.

I lost my mother's watch. And look! my last, or
next-to-last, of three loved houses went.
The art of losing isn't hard to master.

I lost two cities, lovely ones. And, vaster,
some realms I owned, two rivers, a continent.
I miss them, but it wasn't a disaster.

—Even losing you (the joking voice, a gesture
I love) I shan't have lied. It's evident
the art of losing's not too hard to master
though it may look like (*Write* it!) like disaster.

Any villanelle, by its recursive form, imitates an unrelenting
process. The classic villanelle exhibits two recurrent lines, but
Bishop repeats merely one line in its entirety and uses for the
second repeating unit a single word, "disaster"; the whole poem
is, in fact, a duel between the verb "master" and the noun "disaster." Thirteen variants of the word "lose" come into view, to in-
tensify the glare of the formal repetitions of stoic line and menacing word. (Even *lost*'s phonetic sibling *last* is twice pressed
into service.) "Is it hard to master the art of losing?" the poem
asks, and throughout (until the last stanza), Bishop answers,
sometimes impertinently, sometimes defiantly, "No," instancing
cases where she mastered that art in the past by refusing to resort to the word "disaster." But when the new threat of the loss
of her lover makes the poet ask "Is it now *too* hard to master the
art of losing?" she almost falters into "Yes," ready to relinquish
the struggle, ready in fact to give up on a life that seems already
lost. Although Bishop's emotional fragility has made each life-
loss in fact catastrophic, she has, to prove her stoicism, refused
so far to capitulate to despair.

Stoicism is usually thought of as a virtue, but not as an art.
What turns losing into the art of losing? What turns life into

the art of life, writing into the art of writing? This is a question to which Bishop in the course of *Geography III* gives multiple answers, some benign, some much less so. In her late *ars poetica* "Poem," life turns into art when "life, and the memory of it," are preserved in a recognizable painting of a loved place, even if the painting itself is materially "worthless." But in another late poem, "Pink Dog," art is the *fantasía*, or carnival costume, that will cover up the scabies of a diseased post-partum dog, preventing its being thrown (with the other ill and poor of Río) into the river. Art in Río's carnival is a mask to overcome social unacceptability. In a disturbing moment in yet another poem from *Geography III*, "Crusoe in England," art is a death-dealing experiment in the unnatural; Crusoe on his island dyes a baby goat red, "just to see something a little different." Bishop reports the outcome obliquely: "And then his mother wouldn't recognize him." We are left to imagine the baby goat's dying from the dyeing. Art in Crusoe's hands is heedless of its effects, a dilettante's dabbling. What sort of art, by comparison to these, is "the art of losing"? Hard to master, it does not come naturally. It is not spontaneously inventive, like the dyeing of the goat, nor socially deceptive, like the *fantasía*. It does not come with conventions, as the art of even the bad painting of "Poem" does. Nor can the art of losing be taught; it must be self-learned through trial and stoic determination. The art of losing is, however, a form of constantly increasing mastery (unlike the one-time *fantasía*, unlike Crusoe's whimsical fatal experiment, unlike even the amateurish canvas of "Poem").

From being an apprentice in loss, one grows, with practice, to become a master in the art of losing. What happens if a master such as Bishop refuses the next offered advance in mastery? Her hard-won self-image of capability and power will vanish, and she will once again be the poor frightened creature she was when she first confronted loss. In defending her painfully composed self, constructed over time and against daunting losses (beginning with the death of her father when she was eight months old), Bishop—whose catastrophes have made her define life as a constant denuding—must take the next step of mastery. If she does not, she will experience not only the anticipated erotic loss but, even worse, the inner death characteristic of a failed artist. By bringing "One Art" down to the very moment of present writing, by lifting her pen after she writes "like" and then reinscribing "like" after her tenacious interpolation of self-command "(*Write* it!)," Bishop turns once again to the one art she has claimed to master: stoicism in the face of what seems certain ruin. Her art, wrung from loss, paradoxically becomes her life principle. It is not, however, a boast of conclusive mastery of loss that closes the poem; it is merely the recognition of imminent dissolution, a potential arrival at the worst. The conscious recognition of threat is the prelude—the necessary prelude—to any act of mastery over loss. Bishop readies herself, with her self-injunction in the actual moment of composition, to take a step toward a continued writing life, even as we feel her undertow of panic. Nowhere in Bishop's work has the full binocular vision of the coexistence of living and losing been harder to maintain.

An even more desperate, and consequently nearly non-binocular, poem in *Geography III* is "Night City," subtitled "From the Plane."[7] As Bishop's airborne speaker looks down on a lighted city at night, Bishop's imagination creates, for her gaze, the panorama of a hellish purgatory. The city burns, burns with fires, burns with liquids, and then begins to burn as a "guilt-disposal" station. Blood and lymph spatter out; molten green rivers run through the scene; a pool of bitumen resembles a blackened moon. A skyscraper drips incandescent wires;

the air diminishes to a vacuum, the sky is dead. All this is reminiscent of the lake of burning marl on which Milton placed Satan, but here no living beings can, it seems, survive, since the "guilt-disposal" furnace-city generates such intense heat. Bishop offers a quasi-posthumous vision from above of the place in which mortal guilt is punished, futile tears incinerated.

"Night City" is weighted cruelly toward death, until at the last moment the last stanza creates a second view. Can a concept of life persist beside this concept of a hellish purgation? Here are the first nine stanzas of "Night City," with Bishop's speaker shrinking, safe in the aircraft above, from what it would be to walk the landscapes of the "night city," where even tycoons cannot defeat the fires, and where (in a reminiscence of Moore's "the chasm side is // dead") we find "the sky is dead":

> No foot could endure it,
> shoes are too thin.
> Broken glass, broken bottles,
> heaps of them burn.
>
> Over those fires
> no one could walk:
> those flaring acids
> and variegated bloods.
>
> The city burns tears.
> A gathered lake
> of aquamarine
> begins to smoke.
>
> The city burns guilt.
> —For guilt-disposal
> the central heat
> must be this intense.

Diaphanous lymph,
bright turgid blood,
spatter outward
in clots of gold

to where run, molten
in the dark environs
green and luminous
silicate rivers.

A pool of bitumen
one tycoon
wept by himself,
a blackened moon.

Another cried
a skyscraper up.
Look! Incandescent,
its wires drip.

The conflagration
fights for air
in a dread vacuum.
The sky is dead.

Even grand human effort has expired in uselessness; one ty-coon ended by weeping black tears, another's skyscraper has short-circuited its wiring. Bishop is the protected tour guide above, saying "Look!" as she enumerates the sights of the con-flagration below; but she has also been, evidently, the sufferer who in the past has lived in this city, can imagine its shards of glass abrading her feet as she recoils from its broken bottles, its mounting fires, the approaching vacuum in the atmosphere. She has fled the city of guilt and passion and sees from afar its apocalyptic conflagration in a dead sky. She has escaped into a higher realm of the atmosphere, from which her commentary emanates.

Yet, to close the poem, she resumes her former position in the terrible night city, counting on the winged creatures above, the angel aircraft overhead, to set a norm that implicitly judges the deadly sins being purged in the Night City. The guardians above are aware, and obedient, and careful; they know how to follow the necessary laws of stop and go; their steps are regular and measured. The last stanza, imitating the steady stepping of the airplane angels, declares,

> (Still, there are creatures,
> careful ones, overhead.
> They set down their feet, they walk
> green, red; green, red.)

The careful creatures are the incarnation of a moral order rebuking the guilts of earth, but their passionlessness and carefulness cannot compete in vividness with the incandescent fires of the burning city, its unlimited fuel of tears. The angelic moral order above is a life-serenity posed, in this "posthumous" view, at an interface with a purgatorial punishment below. Yet Bishop cannot finish her poem from her observation post in the heaven overhead; her final look at the planes is taken from the excruciating vantage point of the suffering city. The solution offered in the final stanza is an ingenious one: the poet aspires to, and even admires, the steadiness of a moral order, but remains unable to speak from its privileged position, superior to careless mistake-making life. In its imbalance of death and life, "Night City" is the least "just" of Bishop's binocular views; nonetheless, in spite of her shame and terror, the poet gives the last word to the providential surveillance of disorderly passionate life by a principle of temperance overhead.

Years before *Geography III*, in "At the Fishhouses," Bishop made a vow to know what there was to be known, even if it tasted bitter, then briny, then burned the tongue. As her own mortality began to shadow her perpetual delight in her "stereoscopic view"—as she called it in "Cape Breton"—she courageously allowed death to preempt one half of that view. Pressing her style to the extreme, she conveyed authentically the moral stereoscopy of life being lived in the expectation of death. A desolate and convincing binocular picture appears in Bishop's superb imagining of her own grief-ridden state in "Crusoe in England." To the aged returned Crusoe, everything that had meaning on his island has in England lost its significance:

> I'm old.
> I'm bored, too, drinking my real tea,
> surrounded by uninteresting lumber.
> The knife there on the shelf—
> it reeked of meaning, like a crucifix.
> It lived. How many years did I
> beg it, implore it, not to break?
> I knew each nick and scratch by heart,
> the bluish blade, the broken tip,
> the lines of wood-grain on the handle . . .
> Now it won't look at me at all.
> The living soul has dribbled away.

In such a passage, we see Bishop's late binocular capacity at its strongest as she conjoins, in a single comprehensive last look, the living knife on the island, "reek[ing] of meaning," and the same knife soul-less in England. The emotional death of Crusoe's own soul is revealed a little later: "—And Friday, my dear Friday, died of measles / seventeen years ago come March." The date on which Friday died in the flesh is the date that Crusoe died in spirit. Nothing in the knife itself has changed, but the atmosphere in Crusoe's mind has altered beyond repair. In his mind, as in Bishop's last book, life and death, the island and the shelf, exist side by side, before the eye and within the style.

_____

Self-Portraits While Dying: James Merrill
and *A Scattering of Salts*

By the time James Merrill was writing his last volume, *A Scattering of Salts* (1995), he had been ill for several years with
AIDS. And although he died of a heart attack after treatment
for an infection, death by one cause or another was not, as he
knew, far off. *A Scattering of Salts* is suffused with forms of farewell in many lyric genres, including several last looks by the
poet at himself. When we think of successive self-portraits in
painting, Rembrandt is the model; but unlike a painter, a poet
is not restricted in self-portraiture to depicting only the visible
parts of the body, nor is he limited to one moment of expression. Merrill can give us microscopic views of his diseased cells,
films of his flickering consciousness, witty life histories. The
painfulness of drawing a self-portrait in age is exacerbated in
Merrill's case by an ill man's graying flesh, gaunt body, and halt-
ing pace. The genre becomes especially difficult to one so sus-
ceptible to the beautiful as Merrill was, to one so handsome as
Merrill had been. At the same time, since in age and illness
(barring dementia) one is as much alive in consciousness as
ever, the self-portrait must find a stylistic equivalent for the
quickness of the senses and the spirit even as the deathly dissolution of the body becomes certain.

Drawing a self-portrait in verse is attended by three problems common to all verse: finding a symbolic mode, determining adequate external and internal verse forms, and achieving

an appropriate tonality. What might be the symbolic, prosodic, and structural forms "matching" the state of the diseased body? And how might such forms be confronted in a single poem by counter-forms "matching" the continuation of vivacity in the undiseased mind? Are there forms in which failing body and witty mind—at this stage so self-contradictory—can be simultaneously contained? Self-elegy requires lament, but a volume full of laments would not sufficiently embody the extended range of tonalities, from the frivolous to the tragic, natural to Merrill. And elegy requires mourners; but who will mourn the childless poet? And finally, can the modern poet command the apotheosis—the joyful rebirth—that used to be called into play to conclude both the classical and the Christian elegy, in which a second immortal portrait can replace the mortal initial one as, in "Lycidas," the drowned youth becomes both a saint in heaven and classical genius of the shore?

Merrill's very last self-portrait, written too late for inclusion in *A Scattering of Salts*, invents a harrowingly graphic way, using the genre of the shaped poem, of dealing with the problems I have sketched. Called "Christmas Tree"[1] and reproduced at the beginning of chapter 1, it is not Merrill's only visually emblematic late self-portrait; we will here encounter two others, one called "Pearl" and the other "b o d y." But the graphic tactic of "Christmas Tree" is a drastic one, as those of "Pearl" and "b o d y" are not: the entire left half of "Christmas Tree" is visibly missing on the page.[2] The sliced-in-half shape declares the first truths of the poem: that the tree is already dead, having been cut down, and that the missing left half of the tree is its ghost. Yet by bestowing voice on the remaining half-shape, Merrill emphasizes a simultaneous counter-truth: that the tree, with its gleaming green needles, gives every appearance of being still alive. The dead-alive tree has watched with both grief and irony as it has been set up in the house and gaily trimmed; yet it is warmed beyond irony by the delight of the admiring children (who do not realize they, and their mother, are its mourners). The tree's apotheosis—among ornaments, lights, tinsel, angels, trumpets, and suspended music box—glorifies it in a final radiance as Merrill takes his last look at his already-posthumous self. I will return to this final self-portrait, especially to its sadder moments, at the end of my glances at Merrill's other ventures in the genre of elegiac self-representation.

The predicament of being to all appearances alive while having received a death sentence became widely visible in society with the advent of AIDS in its first, lethal form. In his last few years, while composing the poems of *A Scattering of Salts*, Merrill preferred to live his public life as a person who appeared healthy, if frail, while with private knowledge he expected death at any time. This double life awakened galvanizing metaphors within Merrill's self-portraits, and we must remember that for poets metaphors are not "figures of speech" or rhetorical adornments; they are the precise and literal truth of feeling, voiced as closely as the poet can approximate it. Merrill's many metaphors for his dead-alive state in his self-portraits carry him down through his own imagined death, and even past it, until, in "A Look Askance"—a poem written in tercets hinting at Dante's *terza rima* of the afterlife—the poet's poem is seen posthumously as a fossil.

"A Look Askance" begins, however, at the onset of fatal illness: some day soon, a firestorm set going by an unseen hand at "the topmost outlet" of the sky will result in the destruction of Merrill's body, here imagined as a city. At the moment of incinerating heat, filaments of the poet's globe-shaped brain, like those of an enlarged electric bulb, will burn out, as a whole "city-wide brainstorm" overwhelms all cognitive circuits and their codes, setting "loop, dot, dash, node, filament / Inside the vast gray-frosted bulb ablaze." The poet's sense of time's acceleration with the approach of death provokes a demented creativity:

> When the confetti
> Punctuation, the tickertape neologisms begin to pour
> From the mad speed-writer plugged into the topmost
> outlet,
>
> Will it be heat of his—our—bright idea
> Makes that whole citywide brainstorm incandesce,
> Sets loop, dot, dash, node, filament
>
> Inside the vast gray-frosted bulb ablaze?—
> The fire-fonts, the ash script descending
> Through final drafts of a sentence
>
> Passed upon us even as we pass into this
> Fossil state thought up, then idly
> Jotted down on stone.

In this first cascade of metaphor (the death sentence, the crematorium, the ash descending through up-"drafts" of air), the unseen hand above ignites creativity, then revises the script into ash as the death sentence, one of incineration, is carried out. But in Merrill's second fantasy, the hand revises us, after our burial underground, into a fossil replica in stone of our earlier organic form. Merrill himself is here reviving the Horatian prophecy of the poet's script surviving in a form more lasting than bronze; but here not the power of verse, but the power of the grim natural pressure of aeons creates the buried surviving fossil script, "jotted down" posthumously by the unseen hand. The balance of form within the poem incarnates both fantasies: the rapid incandescence into ash is mimicked by the pell-mell cascade of verbs and nouns, while the devolution into fossil imprint is conveyed by the slowed pacing of the final sentence fragment, with its apposition, commas, and repetitions. The fire-fonts of the ash script descend through drafts of a written sentence, which becomes a judicial sentence passed upon us as we harden into buried fossilized form. An individual species has been "thought up," by evolution, and then—by the whimsical choice of an indifferent nature—preserved by being "jotted down" on stone.

Such strikingly original self-portraits-while-dying as the Christmas tree or the fossil appear in many of the briefer poems of *A Scattering of Salts*. From them, I choose a few of Merrill's more ambitious ones: "Alabaster," "The Instilling," "Pearl," "b o d y," "Self-Portrait in Tyvek™ Windbreaker," "An Upward Look," and, at the end, "Christmas Tree" again. In each case, I'll consider the poem in the light of the predicament confronting an artist, simultaneously alive and dead, when he asks by what forms he can represent, in a single last look, the conditions and emotions of his final state.

In the most chilling of these self-portraits, "Alabaster," the poet (as human being) has already died. Although at some earlier moment, a biopsied portion of his still healthy body had been put on a slide for histoscopic examination ("Defenseless, the patrician cells await / Invasion by barbaric viruses"), now his dead flesh, white as alabaster, has been sliced by a microtome into thin sections for a pathologist's inspection that will reveal the life-disease of the corpse. (Needless to say, the poet imagines himself not only as the dead tissue but also as the coroner scrutinizing the slide through his microscope as he pursues his "pious autopsy.") In the pitiless light affixing its beam, the poet can see, memorialized in the flesh, each crucial episode of his past life; it is as if

> a tissue-thin
> Section of self lay on a lighted slide,
> And a voice breathed in your ear,
> "Yes, ah yes. That red oxide
> Stain is where your iron, Lady Hera,
> Entered him."

But is there any point, the poet asks himself, in contemplating a life wound, no matter how vivid, after death? Rather, the dying but living Merrill, his past still painfully sharp, forgoes leisurely inspection of memories in favor of a grim rendition of the moment at which the lucid molecules of the organic self will have been "decrystallized" by death fever into the now inorganic matter under microscopic inspection—no longer the titular "noble" alabaster but instead the more friable chalk:

> Nor will the self resist,
> Broken on terror like a rack,
> When waves of nightmare heat decrystallize
> Her lucid molecules to chalk.

Form is so important to Merrill that he cannot imagine becoming formless, cannot watch his orderly crystalline alabaster *anima* being tortured into decrystallization. (The fear of decrystallization is soothed, as we shall see, only in "An Upward Look," the poem that closes *A Scattering of Salts*.) Yet the formless "chalk" that remains at the end of life is the material of the earliest school-writing instrument, and will enable, imaginatively, the reinscription of the poet's work on the child's first writing surface, a slate.

"Alabaster" is the harshest of the "posthumous" poems, and the one with the least time given to the living self. Among the self-portraits depicting the poet as still alive, the sonnet "The

Instilling" is the most mysteriously beautiful. It is an "inside view," a cinematic portrait of an illuminated spirit descending through a vertical human body that is conceived partly as architecture, partly as organic nature. The trepanned skull of the poet's body resembles the dome of the Pantheon, with a roof oculus allowing rays of light to penetrate; there is a vertebral stair down from the brain through the body, but on that stair the light may be sometimes blurred by the red fog of disturbing emotion emitted by the heart. Within the interior space of the body, "tendoned glades" are visible, the haunt of former lovers "who came and went." Agitated now, the light that is being instilled into the body becomes a cone-shaped spotlight, a "manic duncecap"; the spirit, rebelling against the new philosophic knowledge being insistently instilled, becomes a whirling "danseuse" eluding the searching spotlight. Finally, in grief, the spirit becomes frail, grasping the newel bone of the spine in its tense tight-lipped descent. We move in concert with Merrill's light-of-new-knowledge as it enters by way of the brain and, proceeding in its vertical downward journey through flesh and bone, instills itself into the inmost parts of the self. But suddenly there comes a terrifying blackout when the light becomes "invisible," when illumination not only ceases but seems to have departed for good. The poet's pen halts at that point, when the agitated pangs of the spirit and the increasing frailty of the body produce a muting effect even on consciousness. The creative light that "should" remain unimpeded even in the sick body seems, dangerously, to fail. Here is "The Instilling," its interwoven rhymes mimicking the wayward motion of its inner light:

> All day from high within the skull
> Dome of a Pantheon, trepanned—light shines
> Into the body. Down that stair

Sometimes there's fog: opaque red droplets check
The beam. Sometimes tall redwood-tendoned glades
Come and go, whose dwellers came and went.
Now darting feverishly anywhere,
Manic duncecap its danseuse eludes,

Now slowed by grief, white-lipped,
Grasping the newel bone of its descent,

This light can even be invisible.

The sonnet needs three more lines. In its descent down the page, it has been reticent about the violent means by which the instilling of light was made possible—a surgical trepanning of the closed skull, exposing the naked brain. Just as the abyss of despair opens, with the body violated and the light invisible, just as this self-portrait of brain consciousness "dies," "a deep sparkle" in the heart, as carefully articulated as script, as revelatory of heartbeat as an EKG, awakens once again the poet's sexual longing for the sleeping body next to him. The sparkle defines a field of emotion revealed by a virtual scan of the heart within the inner space:

This light can even be invisible

Till a deep sparkle, regular as script,
As wavelets of an EKG, defines
The dreamless gulf between two shoulder blades.

In constructing self-portraits, Merrill has determined that the investigative light beam of death-awakened consciousness, checked and driven by dread and love, has as much right to be portrayed, in its final days, as the visible body. The sonnet, as unpredictable as consciousness itself, is elusive, divided into irregular stanzas (though the final three-line grouping mirrors the three-line opening one), and unforeseeable in its rhyming (it includes two unrhymed lines and separates the other rhymes, often widely, from each other). The end of the poem at first resists interpretation as it announces, with palpable relief, the unexpected return of the light in a "deep sparkle" of unknown origin; but by comparing the sparkle to the EKG that registers the heart's fluctuations, Merrill prepares us for the sonnet's final gaze at the dreamlessly material body of the beloved. In part because it *is* a sonnet—that paradigmatic form of love poetry—this transgressive sonnet resolves itself traditionally in reawakened passion, as a new light, emblem of the living heart, coexists with the fever and hopelessness of dying.

Like "The Instilling," "Pearl" represents mind at the end of life. The mind here has perfected itself not as an alabaster crystal lattice, nor as an insistent beam of light, but as a pearl, gradually accumulating concentric layers over a lifetime. Merrill begins the poem in his boyhood when he sees, with wonder, on an almost invisible slender chain around his mother's neck, the "real, deepwater" pearl that he has now, after her death, inherited. Just as the oyster, difficult of access in its deepwater hiding place, gradually surrounds its original irritant with a secretion, covering a piece of "grit" with layer upon nacreous layer, so the mind accretes material around an original site of trauma and becomes in its turn the "Pearl" of Merrill's title. I said earlier that "Pearl," like "Christmas Tree," resorts to graphic means to form its self-portrait. But whereas "Christmas Tree" (since it is a self-portrait as fatally ill body) must show itself to be half ghost, markedly less than whole, "Pearl," the poem of the ultimate attainment of the undiseased mind, is beautiful and complete, brought to utter rondure. In "Pearl," Merrill signifies this concentration of layers, and this perfection of a sphere, by his symmetrically concentric rhyme scheme:

PEARL

Well, I admit
A small boy's eyes grew rounder and lips moister
To find it invisibly chained, at home in the hollow
Of his mother's throat: the real, deepwater thing.
Far from the mind at six to plumb
X-raywise those glimmering lamplit
Asymmetries to self-immolating mite
Or angry grain of sand
Not yet proverbial. Yet his would be the hand
Mottled with survival—
She having slipped (how? when?) past reach—
That one day grasped it. Sign of what
But wisdom's trophy. Time to mediate,
Skin upon skin, so cunningly they accrete,
The input. For its early mote
Of grit
Reborn as orient moon to gloat
In verdict over the shucked, outsmarted meat . . .
One layer, so to speak, of calcium carbonate
That formed in me is the last shot
—I took the seminar I teach
In Loss to a revival—
Of Sacha Guitry's classic *Perles de la Couronne*.
The hero has tracked down
His prize. He's holding forth, that summer night,
At the ship's rail, all suavity and wit,
Gem swaying like a pendulum
From his fing—oops! To soft bubble-blurred harpstring
Arpeggios regaining depths (man the camera, follow)
Where an unconscious world, my yawning oyster,
Shuts on it.

Around the central word for trauma, "grit" (which rhymes not only with the first line's "admit" and the last line's "it," but also with the inner rhymes "lamplit" and "wit"), Merrill builds up a series of mirroring end rhymes. Flanking "grit" at the very center are "mote" and "gloat"; the next inner layer rhymes "accrete" and "meat," and so on, until the almost-perfect pearl is built up through fifteen layers of often gifted rhyme ("moister" and "oyster"; "meat" and "accrete"; "*Couronne*" and "down"). I say that the pearl of the poem is "almost perfect" because the concentric single-line rhyme scheme is broken by the appearance of the adjacent double rhymes "sand" and "hand" in the first half, matching the adjacent double rhymes "*Couronne*" and "down" in the second. But since these couplets match each other, fore and aft, concentricity has not, after all, been abandoned. By this departure from a perfect concentricity, Merrill has included, in his pearl, a verbal version of the "asymmetries" visible in his mother's jewel.

Just as his mother "slipped . . . past reach" in death, so the poet sees his own consciousness awaiting its disappearance. "Pearl" borrows for its death scene (as Merrill tells us) the closing frame of Sacha Guitry's film *Les Perles de la Couronne*, in which the hero (whose "suavity and wit," ironically mentioned, cannot prevent failure) loses a pearl when it slips from his fingers into the ocean. The occasional asymmetries of the real pearl's layers are imitated in Merrill's poem not only in the matched doubled rhymes early and late, but also in the asymmetries of line length: the lines range in length from one beat to five, with lines of two, three, and four beats scattered throughout the poem in an imitation of spontaneous and unpredictable recollection and accretion over time. Although, as I have said, the life-theme of Merrill's self-portrait in "Pearl" is the gem-like perfecting of the inner consciousness by the accretion of "skins" of response over a lifetime, the dying body resists this consoling thought, just as the opaque red of anger or love could fog the persistent light in "The Instilling." The mortal body of the poet—the death-theme of the self-portrait—is evoked at the very center of the poem in the form of the dying oyster's flesh, from which the pearl has been plucked. The original "mote / Of grit" is "reborn" as a pearl, "as orient moon to gloat / In verdict over the shucked, outsmarted meat. . . ." The lunar immortality of art (and the fascination of the precious bequest from mother to son) remains, but the beauty of the inner pearl of consciousness is shadowed by the poet's anger on behalf of the lifeless body, seen coarsely as "meat" once it has been "shucked" and "outsmarted" by death, or art. A perfected consciousness does not preclude the poet's "seminar . . . / In Loss," the death-theme being taught to others through his art. His hand—that inscribing instrument of mind—is "mottled," not only by age and perhaps illness, but also by survival through successive painfully maculate "asymmetries" of inner identity. By preserving the presence of the insulted body in his self-por-traits—however full of light or glimmering gems those poems may be—Merrill makes them credible performances of a being intensely alive yet aware of ghastly dissolution.

The most "literary" of the self-portraits of dissolution is the gentle two-stanza account in "b o d y" of how "*body* shines / no longer." Using graphic means once again, as in "Christmas Tree" and "Pearl," Merrill imagines the "o" of the word "body" as a lu-nar eye/I, "a little kohl-rimmed moon" (the kohl being the thickened part of the letter "o"), which rises from the right-rounded base of "b," makes its way to its apogee in "o," and sets in the left-rounded base of "d." That is the little moon's total alphabetic life journey—a three-letter span. Merrill, feeling the pang of the body's brevity, asks the universal question: "Why?" He lets the first stanza spill over into the second to pose that protesting question:

BODY

Look closely at the letters. Can you see,
entering (stage right), then floating full,
then heading off—so soon—
how like a little kohl-rimmed moon
o plots her course from *b* to *d*

—as *y*, unanswered, knocks at the stage door?

The word "body," like all words, becomes, as death approaches,
a lifeless thing, disintegrating into its mere component letters
until it becomes meaningless. "Looked at too long, words fail, /
phase out." But in the failure of semantic meaning (the "plot-
ting" of its course from word to word by the little moon), a new
alphabetic code arises, as the word "body" separates itself into
an assemblage of distinct graphic signs:

Looked at too long, words fail,
phase out. Ask, now that *body* shines
no longer, by what light you learn these lines
and what the *b* and *d* stood for.

The light of sense goes out, says Wordsworth, "with a flash that
[reveals] / The invisible world" (*The Prelude* [1850] VI, lines
601–2). That unprecedented flash of new light gives access to a
revelatory knowledge, and by the light of that philosophical
lesson, one learns the ultimate question: what did the *b* and
d—one's birth and death—stand for?

   The disposition of rhymes in "b o d y"—*abcca* in each
stanza—makes its beautiful effect only when one sees that the
b-rhyme "full" of the floating moon in stanza one matches the
extinguishing *b*-rhyme "fail" of stanza two. Something, Merrill
implies, connects fullness and failing: in each case, a light
shines, first the light of sense and then the light of wisdom. The

initial pathos of the poem—the sweetness of the little kohl-rimmed eye-moon and her eclipse as she utters her plaintive "Why?"—turns bracing as the poet commands himself (and ourselves with him, by his second-person address) to elucidate, by a more philosophical light, what his span of life stood for. Once read, this little poem is impossible to forget, its graphic drama so visibly, but unobtrusively, carried out, its linking slant rhyme of "full" and "fail" so touching, its little moon of sense so prematurely eclipsed—"so soon"—as it bestows by its disappearance the enlightenment of self-understanding.

But pathos is by no means the tone of all the self-portraits in *A Scattering of Salts*. The poem that drew me to Merrill's dying self-representations—his "Self-Portrait in Tyvek™ Windbreaker"—poses its self-portrait before a panorama of absurd and dangerous contemporary items against which Merrill's sardonic wit and self-irony are allowed full play. We are charmed by what the poet has substituted for the traditional white shroud—a white windbreaker (printed with a multicolored world map) that serves to hide the "blood-red T-shirt" underneath, representing the flayed body of the dying poet as *écorché*. Merrill bought his Tyvek™ windbreaker in an eco-friendly shop, its New Age wares summed up in one of the poet's many comic lists:

> I found it in one of those vaguely imbecile
> Emporia catering to the collective unconscious
> Of our time and place. This one featured crystals,
> Cassettes of whalesong and rain-forest whistles,
> Barometers, herbal cosmetics, pillows like puffins,
> Recycled notebooks, mechanized Lucite coffins
> For sapphire waves that crest, break, and recede,
> As they presumably do in nature still.

The context for this self-portrait is the America of the poet's last days, especially its absurdities of matter and manner, which, though alien to the discriminating sensibility of the poet, are in "the collective unconscious" entirely familiar to him, as they are to all Americans. Wearing his worldly (and ridiculously trademarked) windbreaker and his headphoned Walkman, Merrill goes to the gym playing a CD of a Neapolitan singer of the 1940s, Roberto Murolo. Yet the singing voice cannot shut out the external world, and Merrill continues to be preoccupied by America, now by the contemporary ruining of the environment—a parallel to the illness of his own body. Even the cannibals of the past, he thinks, "honored the gods of Air and Land and Sea," but we,

> We though . . . Cut to dead forests, filthy beaches,
> The can of hairspray, oil-benighted creatures,
> A star-scarred x-ray of the North Wind's lungs.

Although the blighted landscape, set against the New Age store, is a further backdrop for this self-portrait-at-the-end-of-days, it is not the final one: the lurid apocalypse of an afflicted, even dying, earth brings on, in reaction, Merrill's comic sense. Aware that a poem displaying only America's science boutiques and eco-sins would not represent his country broadly enough, Merrill begins a far-ranging comic scan of the clichés (journalistic, political, and linguistic) of the current scene, from mall bookstores to phone sex to ketchup as food to TV to Capitol Hill to identity groups:

> Still, not to paint a picture wholly black,
> Some social highlights: Dead white males in malls.
> Prayer breakfasts. Pay-phone sex. "Ring up as meat."
> Oprah. The GNP. The contour sheet.

The painless death of History. The stick
Figures on Capitol Hill. Their rhetoric,
Gladly—no, rapturously (on Prozac) suffered!
Gay studies. Right to Lifers. The laugh track.

Even the presence of death cannot suspend Merrill's custom-
ary mockery. Nor does it alter his impatience: the informality
of the democracy surrounding him temporarily annoys the
poet, as passersby from street workers to foreigners feel free to
comment on his conspicuous jacket; one girl, wearing an identical jacket, even gives him a conspiratorial wave. For all his ir-
ritation, he returns her wave "like an accomplice," with a philosophical reflection:

For while all humans aren't
Countable as equals, we must behave
As if they were, or the spirit dies (Pascal).

This Pascalian conviction—that his fellow human beings are,
after all, his moral equals—rules Merrill's culture-scanning
self-portrait, written from the acute vantage point of the disease that at last allies the wealthy and fastidious poet with ev-
eryone mortal. As a sign of approaching death, the trendy
white shroud-jacket now seems inadequate, and reflecting on
the rapidity with which styles fall out of fashion, Merrill decides to pack it away—"Not throwing out [the] motley once
reveled in" of his more carefree past, but "just learning to live
down the wrinkled friend" (his old and ill physical self) that
had inhabited the white world-map windbreaker. As Merrill
wonders what possible verbal garment can suit him for the
obliterating moment to come, he knows it cannot resemble his
former favorite styles of prophetic wisdom and mock naïveté:

Remember the figleaf's lesson. Styles betray
Some guilty knowledge. What to dress ours in—

A seer's blind gaze, an infant's tender skin?
All that's been seen through. The eloquence to come
Will be precisely what we cannot say
Until it parts the lips.

"The eloquence to come" will be the later self-portrait as
Christmas tree, half-real, half-ghost, though Merrill cannot yet
envisage or enact that final denuded and yet ornamental style.
When the poet (resigning his white cover-up) cannot imagine
the style that will better serve as a shroud, what does he see on
a passing youth (headphoned like himself) but a black celestial
twin of his jacket, this one reproducing not a map of the world
but a map of the night sky and the signs of the zodiac:

What then to wear
When—hush, it's no dream! It's my windbreaker
In black, with starry longitudes, Archer, Goat,
Clothing an earphoned archangel of Space,
Who hasn't read Pascal, and doesn't wave....

Reassured by having had revealed to him, by the black-jacketed
archangel, a garment for death not only appropriate but beautiful, the poet can resume listening, on his own headphones, to
the voice of Roberto Murolo. He addresses his fellow singer
directly—"Sing our final air"—and then lets that aria follow as
his closing stanza. This plangent coda issues from a voice already failing, able to utter only broken deathbed words; and yet
we know, since the poem is written in pentameters, that every
line of this stanza must retain the same rhythmic measure,
must have five beats. After gasping out brief phrases, the dying
voice regains, with a final effort, its living powers and is able to
sing its last three lines complete:

Love, grief etc. * * * * for good reason.
Now only * * * * * * * STOP signs.

133

> Meanwhile * * * * * if you or I've ex-
> ceeded our [?] * * * ~~more than time~~ was needed
> To fit a text airless and * * as Tyvek
> With breathing spaces and between the lines
> Days brilliantly recurring, as once *we* did,
> To keep the blue wave dancing in its prison.

Because we can guess how the lines should go thematically, and because Merrill has provided all the rhymes, we of course feel compelled to imagine words that might fill the gaps. Love and grief, in the poet's final aria, are failing because the body is dying; but although all signs point to death and waning creative power, those old emotions of love and grief still supply Merrill's last words to his lover. Here's one metrical reconstruction—not so clever as Merrill would have made it:

> Love, grief etc. failing for good reason,
> Now only does the body wince at STOP signs.
> Meanwhile, dear heart, recall, if you or I've ex-
> ceeded our powers, more than time was needed
> To fit a text airless and taut as Tyvek
> With breathing spaces and between the lines
> Days brilliantly recurring, as once *we* did,
> To keep the blue wave dancing in its prison.

The eco-boutique's blue wave, encased in its Lucite coffin, was moved mechanically, but the motion of spirit in the measure of the poem is aesthetically metrical rather than industrially mechanized. "Wavelets" of the failing heart still dance, coffined in the transparent container of the stanza. Because Merrill, always an introspective poet, had become, by his middle years, a poet of greater world awareness (writing not only of Europe and Greece but also of the Weathermen, terrorism, and the depletion of the earth's resources), he poses himself, in

134

this most densely allusive of his self-portraits, before the landscape of technological American popular culture rather as Caspar David Friedrich, in a sublime mode, would pose one of his solitary figures before a mountain range or a wilderness.

The "final air" in "Self-Portrait in a Tyvek$^{(TM)}$ Windbreaker" subsides to a wistful farewell, easing the reader's passage to the last poem—and the last self-portrait—of *A Scattering of Salts*. By analogy to the opening poem of the volume, called "A Downward Look," Merrill entitles the last poem "An Upward Look." In the course of its nineteen lines, a crystal of salt becomes transformed into the morning star and then the evening star. Apotheosis as stellification is not new (Pope stellified Belinda's hair in *The Rape of the Lock*), but it had never chosen as its vehicle a crystal of salt—the salt of bodily fluids, of tears, of savor. In "An Upward Look"—the poem as lachrymal—the salt goes through several mutations before it attains its final sidereal height. The poet's heart is a field that has been sown with salt (a substance preventing further organic growth) by its "departing occupier," a lover who is already turning away from his dying companion. The salt then metamorphoses into human worth, "salt of the earth," which the poet in defiance has thrown backward for luck but which now resumes its exacerbating sting. How has the whole world metamorphosed into salt, tears, bad luck? The poet's universe has become something like a hospital for the terminally ill, "this vast facility the living come / dearest to die in   How did it happen."

"How did it happen"—the poem's central outcry, its protest at how unexpectedly and strangely living turns to dying—ends the single anomalous stanza of the poem—not a couplet but a tercet—enlarged precisely to make room for that dying question ("How" this time, rather than "Why," as in "b o d y"). This anomaly in stanza-length makes us ask why Merrill had decided in the first place to cast "An Upward Look" in couplets, and why he allowed his symmetry to be broken.[3] Couplet stanzas are the most "primitive" stanza form, suiting the aboriginal and universal events of birth and death. The "extra" line of the lone tercet is there to make room for the poem's sole direct address to another—"dearest"—as well as its harrowing outcry. The form of "An Upward Look" attracts attention not only because of the strange invariant white space separating each line into two half-lines, but also because of the presence of alliterative gestures that recall the half-lines in the accentual meter of Anglo-Saxon poetry. Although Merrill does not entirely obey the rules governing alliteration in Anglo-Saxon poetics, he lets us hear comparable effects (I capitalize the alliterating words or phonemes):

[the lover] finds the world Turning

Toys Triumphs	Toxins into
this VaSt faCiLity	the LiVing come
Dearest to Die in	How did it Happen.

Why might Merrill have recalled the alliterative Anglo-Saxon half-line for his upward-looking farewell to terrestrial life? Perhaps he inserts visual pauses of equal typographical length (not present in Anglo-Saxon poetry) between the two halves of each line to make it seem as though the faltering speaking voice had to restrict itself to short phrases, could not "do" a whole line at once, had to pause for breath. And yet the prominent alliterative links tell us that the infirm speaker wants to defeat those pauses in the middle of each line by emphasizing the aural connections of his half-lines to each other, the sounds that link the halves over the midline break. We can see, too, that Merrill's half-lines anticipate the about-to-appear answer to the baffled question "How did it happen?" "Halves of a clue" approach, half-line by half-line, explaining Merrill's choice of form. But before they can appear and be named, Merrill joyously characterizes the halves of his clue as universal, "bright," and mirrored in every mortal creature's thinking:

In bright alternation	minutely mirrored
within the thinking	of each and every
mortal creature	halves of a clue
approach the earthlights	Morning star
evening star	salt of the sky.

"Bright" evokes "light" as its usual twin, and light is here multiplied into "earthlights," denoting our sun and moon. The halves of a clue are the morning star (heralding the sun) and evening star (heralding the moon). In the light of their "bright alternation," Merrill can turn away from the anger and perplexity of "How did it happen" and find equanimity.

Merrill would have known Sappho's poem to the evening star, and Byron's adaptation of it in the third canto of *Don Juan* (stanza 107),[4] but he depends more intimately here on Tennyson's *In Memoriam* (CXXI), which turns on the fact that the evening star and the morning star are one and the same. Sappho had called the star by its "evening" name, Hesperus, but Tennyson extends the evening star, Hesper, into dawn so that he can address it by its bright "morning" name, Phosphor. In the last stanza of his poem, as his halves come together, Tennyson (like Merrill) unites the star's two alternating self-manifestations in a "double name":

> Sad Hesper o'er the buried sun
> And ready, thou, to die with him,
> Thou watchest all things ever dim
> And dimmer, and a glory done:

The team is loosen'd from the wain,
        The boat is drawn upon the shore;
        Thou listenest to the closing door,
And life is darken'd in the brain.

Bright Phosphor, fresher for the night,
        By thee the world's great work is heard
        Beginning, and the wakeful bird;
Behind thee comes the greater light:

The market boat is on the stream,
        And voices hail it from the brink;
        Thou hear'st the village hammer clink,
And see'st the moving of the team.

Sweet Hesper-Phosphor, double name
        For what is one, the first, the last,
        Thou, like my present and my past,
Thy place is changed; thou art the same.

For Tennyson, the star preserves its past as it ushers in the greater light of the sun, just as for Merrill, the star keeps to its reassuring cycle, appearing morning and evening in its two equally exquisite manifestations. But although Tennyson's cycle ends with the resurrective dawn, Merrill ends with the appearance of the evening star, heralding night. Merrill's presiding deity is, as ever, Venus, goddess of the passions and of the evening star. As day ends, the evening star materializes, the first salt crystal in a sky that will eventually be scattered with salt stars:

                    Morning star

    evening star   salt of the sky
    First the grave   dissolving into dawn

    then the crucial   recrystallizing
    from inmost depths   of clear dark blue.

The "grave dissolving" into dawn is the melancholy dissolution of the body that parallels the morning star's vanishing with the coming of the sun, but it is also the tomb-grave of a life disappearing in the light of a new order. The verb "recrystallizing" reminds us that the evening star is one of Merrill's crystalline symbols of perfection, which always possess the crucial ability to recrystallize as another symbol. We might expect that the last line would praise the renewed presence of the star as evening comes, and so it does, but in an evolutionary way; what is wonderful is the gradual visual materializing, as the last blue of the day begins to darken, of the reconstituted evening star. For Shakespeare, a star was "a jewel hung in ghastly night," but Merrill's star is a glowing presence evolving out of the inmost dark blue depths of its earthly matrix, day.

"Self-Portrait as Star" (as "An Upward Look" might be called) renders without flinching the loss of crystalline form through dissolution, but then predicts a reappearance, from the "inmost depths" of the poet's closing day, of an analogous crystal lattice in the future. The two halves of the clue are named without adornment at first, then grouped under a single name—"salt of the sky"—and only then permitted their two eloquent present participles, the grave dissolving and the crucial recrystallizing. Merrill's belief in crystalline form is such that he could imagine himself only temporarily without it: when his poems become the historical oeuvre we call "Merrill," their form will recrystallize him.

The difficulty of creating believable self-portraits while dying prompted Merrill's imagination to a series of imaginative self-symbols: a piece of dead human tissue under the microscope of an autopsy; a domed and wounded architectural space into which light is painfully instilled over time; an exploding lightbulb; a fossil; a pearl of many glimmering experiential layers; a little I/eye-moon on its journey from birth to death; a poet life-jacketed and death-jacketed; a morning star and an evening star. Aside from the satiric self-portrait of the jacket-wearing poet posed against his era, the other portraits are of things either dead or inorganic. Perhaps an inorganic self-por-trait—of himself in fossilized, concentric, or crystallized form, archaic relic, pearl, or star—seemed to Merrill the most precise way to depict himself enduring, in Keats's words, a "posthu-mous life." Or perhaps a miniaturized form of self-portrait—thinking of oneself as a tiny eye rising and setting, letter to let-ter, in a single word—seemed accurate to one observing his life from the vast distance imposed by a death sentence. Perhaps redefining living consciousness as a light instilled through a wound, drop by drop, seemed fundamentally more truthful, to the dying poet, than rendering a portrait solely of a ruined body.

Each of these imaginings of self brings stylistic conse-quences. A slicing in two will be correct for the already-dead Christmas tree; a concentric rhyme scheme will suit the pearl; a poem in half-lines will suit halves of a clue. A waywardly rhymed sonnet will suit the wayward descending light of philo-sophic consciousness; a playlet showing the word "body" de-taching itself into separate fragments as the body decays will suit the assumption of cosmic distance from one's own fate; as "full" and "fail" are beginning to rhyme, an accelerating and then slowing pace will re-create crematorium incandescence fol-lowed by a death sentence written on stone; and finally a ver-sion of that ceremonious processional stanza, *ottava rima* (but with only four of the eight lines bearing rhyme), will suit the organic living portrait, the poet's last walk wearing his absurd and surreal Tyvek shroud.

I return, as promised, to Merrill's final self-portrait and his last self-symbol—the paradoxically alive/dead, organic/inor-ganic Christmas tree, retaining only half of its body, but still possessing a voice. We hear from that voice a song of the mixed emotions suiting the interface of life and death: a sadness ("it would be only a matter of weeks"); a flinching from the wasting of its physical form ("To have grown so thin. / Needles and bone"); a wincing at its artificial life support by the electric cord ("a primitive IV / To keep the show going"); and yet a sustained gratitude for the warmth of those attending its last appearance.[5]

In Merrill's montage of self-portraits while dying, an array of unforgettable dying and living selves is produced; a gaunt face, a wasting frame, tissue subjected to medical ministrations, a trepanned skull, a beam of light descending throughout a column of flesh, a motley-wearing jester posed against a ruined earth, a pearl of wisdom accreting in the mind, a self posthumously fossilized, a miniature moon setting out and setting. As Merrill takes his last look at himself, body and soul, he leaves it to his penetrating symbols, enacting his state in their wonderfully individual binocular styles, to carry his agony and his alertness, his decrystallization in nightmare heat and the crucial recrystallizing of self in the lasting art that shines only "from inmost depths" of an imaginative life.

Notes

CHAPTER 1

1. Citations of Stevens are by page number from *Wallace Stevens: Collected Poetry and Prose* (New York: Library of America, 1997).

2. James Merrill, *Collected Poems*, ed. J. D. McClatchy and Stephen Yenser (New York: Alfred A. Knopf, 2001), 866.

3. Emily Dickinson, *Poems*, ed. R. W. Franklin (Cambridge, MA: Belknap Press of Harvard University Press, 1999), 219–20.

4. George Herbert, *Works*, ed. F. E. Hutchinson (Oxford: Clarendon Press, 1941), 185.

5. Christopher Ricks, ed., *The Oxford Book of English Verse* (Oxford: Oxford University Press, 1999), 159. I have modernized Waller's *o're* to *o'er* and his *Let's* to *Lets*.

6. John Donne, *The Complete English Poems of John Donne*, ed. C. A. Patrides (London: J. M. Dent and Sons, 1985), 488–89. I have regularized the different spellings ("streights," "straights," "straits") of this one word, and have departed from Patrides when manuscript variants noted by Patrides warrant it.

7. When I rewrite a line, for purposes of illustration, I enclose that alternative invented line in square brackets.

CHAPTER 2

1. Wallace Stevens, *Letters*, ed. Holly Stevens (New York: Alfred A. Knopf, 1966), 953. Hereafter abbreviated as *L*. Further citations appear parenthetically in the text.

2. For the pool of pink water lilies and the beloved by the poet's side, see the back glance in "Le Monocle de Mon Oncle," XI; for the "turban," see the "caftan" of the "Chieftain" (the large rooster) in "Bantams in Pine-Woods"; for Stevens's passage beyond an aesthetic of greenhouse-cultivated flowers, see "Floral Decorations for Bananas"; for the chimney, see Stevens's frequent later self-descriptions (for example, in "Local Objects") as a spirit "without a foyer." Stephen Burt, who has discovered the actual state of Elizabeth Park in Stevens's late years, describes the decaying Pond House in "Wallace Stevens: Where He Lived," *ELH* (forthcoming).

3. *King Lear:* "As flies to wanton boys are we to the gods; / They kill us for their sport." Keats, on the musk rose: when blown, it becomes "the murmurous haunt of flies on summer eves." See also Baudelaire's "La Charogne."

4. This conjecture does not affect the basic premise, or conduct, of the poem, nor what I say about its strategies.

5. In other long-lined poems by Stevens, the extended line serves different purposes—in "Prologues to What Is Possible" the motion of a boat borne forward over the sea; in "The World as Meditation" the waiting of Penelope for the reappearance of Ulysses.

CHAPTER 3

1. Sylvia Plath, *The Collected Poems*, ed. Ted Hughes (New York: Harper Perennial, 1981), 312. All future citations are identified parenthetically by page number in the text.

2. The *disjecta membra* of this poem will become those of Otto Plath in "The Colossus."

3. The 7 lines (out of 126) of "Berck-Plage" in which the first person appears are the following:

> How the sun's poultice draws on my inflammation. . . .
> I have two legs, and I move smilingly.
> Why should I walk. . . .
> I am not a nurse, white and attendant,

I am not a smile. . . .
And my heart too small to bandage their terrible faults.
And I am dark-suited and still, a member of the party.

4. For Ted Hughes's comments on the visit to Berck-Plage, and for information on the work sheets of "Berck-Plage" (remarking Plath's omission, in the finished draft, of a section concerning the birth of her son, Nicholas), see Jack Folsom's study "Death and Rebirth in Sylvia Plath's 'Berck-Plage,'" Temple University (www.sylviaplath.de/plath/jfolsom.html; accessed July 10, 2009). Folsom's view of the poem is not mine. He writes, "'Berck-Plage,' [with its] seemingly unmitigated malaise and funereal gloom, stands in many readers' estimation as one of her heaviest and least appealing works" (1). He claims, however, that "the speaker . . . has risen above the world's tumult and has seen renewal after death . . . ; she has . . . transformed her grief . . . into a life-renewing vision" (9). He bases this view chiefly on the section on the birth of her son, Nicholas, which Plath excised from the poem; Folsom's optimistic view of the final poem seems, in the light of the cut, indefensible.

5. Tim Kendall, *Sylvia Plath: A Critical Study* (London: Faber and Faber, 2001), 205.

6. The idea of reading a reflection as a "nether world" may have come from Wordsworth's nocturne "Composed by the Side of Grasmere Lake," in which, after seeing the lake as a mirror reflecting the stars, Wordsworth drops into a darker speculation concerning Nature:

Is it a mirror?—or the nether Sphere
Opening to view the abyss in which she feeds
Her own calm fires?

CHAPTER 4

1. Robert Lowell, *Day by Day* (New York: Farrar, Straus and Giroux, 1977), 114. Future references will be identified parenthetically in the text.

2. "Jean Stafford, a Letter," "For John Berryman," "In the Ward," and "The Spell," respectively.

3. Michael Hofmann, "His Own Prophet," *London Review of Books*, September 11, 2003, 3, 5–8.

4. Robert Lowell, *Collected Poems*, ed. Frank Bidart and David Gewanter (New York: Farrar, Straus and Giroux, 2003), 645.

<h2 style="text-align:center">CHAPTER 5</h2>

1. See the volume *Edgar Allan Poe and the Jukebox*, misnamed in its subtitle *Uncollected Poems, Drafts, and Fragments*, ed. Alice Quinn (New York: Farrar, Straus and Giroux, 2006), 158. The word "uncollected" means "not published by the author in book form, but published singly somewhere else, as in a journal." Bishop chose never to publish these drafts of poems at all. "Breakfast Song" was not found among her manuscripts at her death; it had been covertly transcribed from one of her notebooks by Lloyd Schwartz, who released it for publication only after Bishop's death.

2. Page references, here and hereafter given parenthetically, refer to Elizabeth Bishop, *The Complete Poems, 1927–1979* (New York: Farrar, Straus and Giroux, 1983).

3. There is a similar reversal of octave and sestet in Coleridge's "Work without Hope," but the poem retains the pentameter of the traditional sonnet.

4. Bishop is remembering here Shelley's lines in the "Ode on Intellectual Beauty," "Life, like a dome of many-colour'd glass, / Stains the white radiance of Eternity," remembered also in Frost's ice-storm in "Birches," as the ice-bound branches turn "many-colored" when the ice begins to crack in the sun, shedding so many pieces of glassy ice "You'd think the inner dome of heaven had fallen."

5. "Daisies pied" is quoted from Shakespeare's *A Winter's Tale*, "incandescent" from Moore's description of Eden in "Marriage": "Below the incandescent stars / below the incandescent fruit, / the strange experience of beauty."

6. In stanza 1, a trimeter substitutes for one of the pentameters;

in stanza 5, there is a tetrameter substitution. Neither disturbs the contrast between the first four lines of the stanza and the closing hexameter.

7. The compositional history for Bishop's published poems is not yet available. Bishop sometimes waited for years to publish a poem composed long before. It is possible that "Night City" is such a poem; it sounds earlier in style than many other poems in *Geography III* (although the drafts at Vassar are dated 1972). Even if composition had begun earlier, Bishop chose to publish "Night City" in the context of several other poems envisaging the end of life.

CHAPTER 6

1. All references, here and hereafter in parentheses, are to James Merrill's *Collected Poems* (New York: Knopf, 2001).

2. For the complete text of "Christmas Tree," see chapter 1. The poem was published posthumously in 1995 and can be found in Merrill's *Collected Poems*, 866. One printing of the poem, I have been told, did miss the point, centering each line on the page so as to make a symmetrical tree. In writing "Christmas Tree," Merrill may have been remembering another poem about a missing half of oneself, Elizabeth Bishop's "The Gentleman of Shalott." Bishop's male version of the Lady of Shalott is half-real, half-mirrored reflection. The poem ends, "He wishes to be quoted as saying at present: 'Half is enough.'" See Bishop, *Complete Poems*, 10.

3. "An Upward Look" shares these features with its semi-twin, "A Downward Look" (which opens *A Scattering of Salts*); it too is written in couplets, but its symmetry is broken not by a tercet but by one stanza of a single line alone. The asymmetry in each case suggests the imperfection—by excess or defect—of human life.

4. Oh, Hesperus! Thou bringest all good things—
　　Home to the weary, to the hungry cheer,
　To the young bird the parent's brooding wings,
　　The welcome stall to the o'erlabour'd steer;
　Whate'er of peace about our hearthstone clings,

Whate'er our household gods protect of dear,
Are gather'd round us by thy look of rest;
Thou bring'st the child, too, to the mother's breast.

Sappho's poem reads, in a literal translation by Mary Barnard:

Hesperus, you herd
homeward whatever
Dawn's light dispersed

You herd sheep—herd
goats—herd children
home to their mothers.

(*Sappho: A New Translation* [Berkeley:
University of California Press, 1986], 16.)

5. Please refer to Merrill's poem "Christmas Tree" in chapter 1.

The Andrew W. Mellon Lectures in the Fine Arts, 1952–2007

1952 Jacques Maritain, *Creative Intuition in Art and Poetry*
1953 Sir Kenneth Clark, *The Nude: A Study of Ideal Form*
1954 Sir Herbert Read, *The Art of Sculpture*
1955 Etienne Gilson, *Art and Reality* (published as *Painting and Reality*)
1956 E. H. Gombrich, *The Visible World and the Language of Art* (published as *Art and Illusion: A Study in the Psychology of Pictorial Representation*)
1957 Sigfried Giedion, *Constancy and Change in Art and Architecture* (published as *The Eternal Present: A Contribution on Constancy and Change*, 1962)
1958 Sir Anthony Blunt, *Nicolas Poussin and French Classicism*
1959 Naum Gabo, *A Sculptor's View of the Fine Arts* (published as *Of Divers Arts*)
1960 Wilmarth Sheldon Lewis, *Horace Walpole*
1961 André Grabar, *Christian Iconography and the Christian Religion in Antiquity* (published as *Christian Iconography: A Study of Its Origins*)
1962 Kathleen Raine, *William Blake and Traditional Mythology* (published as *Blake and Tradition*)
1963 Sir John Pope-Hennessy, *Artist and Individual: Some Aspects of the Renaissance Portrait* (published as *The Portrait in the Renaissance*)

1964 Jakob Rosenberg, *On Quality in Art: Criteria of Excellence, Past and Present*

1965 Sir Isaiah Berlin, *Sources of Romantic Thought* (published as *The Roots of Romanticism*)

1966 Lord David Cecil, *Dreamer or Visionary: A Study of English Romantic Painting* (published as *Visionary and Dreamer: Two Poetic Painters, Samuel Palmer and Edward Burne-Jones*)

1967 Mario Praz, *On the Parallel of Literature and the Visual Arts* (published as *Mnemosyne: The Parallel between Literature and the Visual Arts*)

1968 Stephen Spender, *Imaginative Literature and Painting*

1969 Jacob Bronowski, *Art as a Mode of Knowledge* (published as *The Visionary Eye*)

1970 Sir Nikolaus Pevsner, *Some Aspects of Nineteenth-Century Architecture* (published as *A History of Building Types*)

1971 T.S.R. Boase, *Vasari: The Man and the Book* (published as *Giorgio Vasari: The Man and the Book*)

1972 Ludwig H. Heydenreich, *Leonardo da Vinci*

1973 Jacques Barzun, *The Use and Abuse of Art*

1974 H. W. Janson, *Nineteenth-Century Sculpture Reconsidered* (published as *The Rise and Fall of the Public Monument*)

1975 H. C. Robbins Landon, *Music in Europe in the Year 1776*

1976 Peter von Blanckenhagen, *Aspects of Classical Art*

1977 André Chastel, *The Sack of Rome: 1527*

1978 Joseph W. Alsop, *The History of Art Collecting* (published as *The Rare Art Traditions: The History of Art Collecting*)

1979 John Rewald, *Cézanne and America* (published as *Cézanne and America: Dealers, Collectors, Artists, and Critics, 1891–1921*)

1980 Peter Kidson, *Principles of Design in Ancient and Medieval Architecture*

1981 John Harris, *Palladian Architecture in England, 1615–1760*

1982 Leo Steinberg, *The Burden of Michelangelo's Painting*

1983 Vincent Scully, *The Shape of France*

2005 Irene Winter, "*Great Work*": *Terms of Aesthetic Experience in Ancient Mesopotamia*

2006 Simon Schama, *Really Old Masters: Age, Infirmity, and Reinvention*

2007 Helen Vendler, *Last Looks, Last Books: The Binocular Poetry of Death* (published as *Last Looks, Last Books: Stevens, Plath, Lowell, Bishop, Merrill*)

Copyright Acknowledgments